MW00454222

God Conflict

Faith in the Face of NEW ATHEISM

PETER FELDMEIER, PHD

Liguori
Liguori, Missouri

Imprimi Potest:
Harry Grile, CSsR, Provincial
Denver Province, The Redemptorists

Published by Liguori Publications
Liguori, Missouri 63057

To order, call 800-325-9521
www.liguori.org

Copyright © 2014 Peter Feldmeier

All rights reserved. No part of this publication may be reproduced, stored in a retrieval system, or transmitted in any form or by any means—electronic, mechanical, photocopy, recording, or any other—except for brief quotations in printed reviews, without the prior written permission of Liguori Publications.

Library of Congress Cataloging-in-Publication Data

Feldmeier, Peter.
The God conflict : faith in the face of new atheism / Peter Feldmeier, PhD.
pages cm
1. Christianity and atheism. 2. Apologetics. I. Title.
BR128.A8F45 2014
239'.7—dc23
2013045125

p ISBN: 978-0-7648-2282-7
e ISBN: 978-0-7648-6892-4

Scripture texts in this work are taken from the *New American Bible*, revised edition © 2010, 1991, 1986, 1970 Confraternity of Christian Doctrine, Washington, D.C., and are used by permission of the copyright owner. All Rights Reserved. No part of the *New American Bible* may be reproduced in any form without permission in writing from the copyright owner.

Excerpts from Vatican documents are used with permission. *Copyright Libreria Editrice Vaticana © Libreria Editrice Vaticana.*

Liguori Publications, a nonprofit corporation, is an apostolate of The Redemptorists. To learn more about The Redemptorists, visit Redemptorists.com.

Printed in the United States of America
18 17 16 15 14 / 5 4 3 2 1
First Edition

Contents

Introduction

An Alarming Movement

The State of Skepticism and New Atheism

In many ways, religion is on the run in the West. While the United States can boast of being the most religious country in Western culture, European Christianity is gasping for air, with dramatically fewer people identifying themselves as Christian, and many of those who do are nominally so at best. Here in the United States, while religious identification is much higher, we have the same problem with shallow commitments. We shouldn't be surprised. Western culture has been on a trajectory of secularization for centuries and religions are by and large marginalized from public discourse. Religious faith is imagined by most, even many religious believers themselves, as something private. Further, locating meaning, truth, value, and so on, are less grounded in religious sensibilities as they are in secular assumptions. John Hick, a noted scholar of religion and culture, has observed:

> *In our Western world, beginning around the seventeenth century, the earlier pervasive religious outlook has increasingly been replaced by an equally pervasive naturalistic outlook, and during the twentieth century this replacement has become almost complete. Naturalism has created a consensus reality of our culture. It has become so ingrained that we no longer see it, but see everything through it.*[1]

Philosopher John Lucas recognized the same thing in terms of scholarly discourse: "Philosophical naturalism is now the orthodoxy of the Western Intellectual world."[2] Religion is simply placed on the safe margins in our society, if it is even addressed at all. Stephen Prothero, in his well-received study on religion in American society, *Religious Literacy*, argues that Americans are Western culture's least knowledgeable about religion. Prothero details that when religion is mentioned in U.S. history schoolbooks, it is often an afterthought or embarrassment.[3] He points out that many world history books even fail to mention the Protestant Reformation or even the life of Jesus. How many Americans were taught that the Great Awakening was the crucial movement that cemented a collective identity among the colonists as a prelude to the Revolutionary War, or that Christian faith was the foundation of the emancipation, temperance, and suffrage movements? When one considers the cultural issues around weak religious commitment, lack of religious literacy, and the marginalization of religion, what we have are the cultural conditions for broad religious skepticism. Poor witness by religious leaders and anti-scientific attitudes among fundamentalist Christians further the problem.

Many sincere religious believers are left with few intellectual resources to respond. When asked by an inquiring skeptic why one should believe in God, a typical response ends up with something that sounds, and may indeed be, gratuitous: faith! But why have faith? What can my faith be grounded in that's reasonable? This is not only a fair question but one that has to be answered with intellectual integrity.

Our current religious state of affairs is even worse off. In the past decade we have seen a spate of books by intellectuals who argue that not only is belief in God irrational, it is downright pernicious. It is the main reason for war, it is anti-scientific, it divides people, and it undermines the truth about who we are.

That's the claim. This has become a bona fide movement, known as New Atheism. In *The Evolution of God*, Robert Wright argues that the culture is shifting toward an anti-religious attitude that is becoming public and aggressive:

> *Indeed, the first decade of the twenty-first century made god-talk an even greater breach of highbrow etiquette than it had been in the twentieth. In the wake of September 11, 2001, anti-religious attitude was central to a slew of influential cultural products (books by Sam Harris, Christopher Hitchens, Daniel Dennett, and Richard Dawkins, a film by Bill Maher, and a one-woman act by Julia Sweeney). In the space of only a few years, the more-or-less official stance of intellectuals toward believers moved from polite silence to open dismissal if not ridicule.*[4]

The four authors Wright cites have sometimes been dubbed "the four horsemen of the apocalypse," given their cultural influence. Dawkins' book *The God Delusion* remained on *The New York Times* bestseller list for fifty-one straight weeks and sold more than 3 million copies worldwide. The authors have been joined by a host of intellectuals from scientific spheres as well as cultural popularizers, including a recent book aimed at *converting* adolescents and young adults to atheism.[5] As we will see, these voices can be quite aggressive. Hitchens considered himself an important crucial voice at a time when "people of faith are in their different ways planning your and my destruction."[6] (I had no idea.) And Harris believes he has penned the most devastating attack on religion *ever*, one that is able "to demolish the intellectual and moral pretensions of Christianity in its most committed forms."[7] Christopher Hitchens died on December 15, 2011, of esophageal cancer. While it might appear unseemly to retort to someone who is no longer alive, the very fact of this famous person's death has increased his book sales, and his books are a central part of the New Atheist landscape. Of course, with all religious people of goodwill, I pray God rest his soul.

Added to these voices are some members of the scientific community who are equally dismissive of religion. They represent a kind of scientific atheism. So the problem isn't only with New Atheism but with a religious skepticism based on principles that both New Atheists and other scientific atheists take as dogma.

Thinking About Reality

New Atheism offers a version of reality. Briefly, it goes like this: *Nothing exists but physical things.* This is their grounding principle, and it is shared by many atheistic philosophers and scientists as well as many religious skeptics: The laws of physics and chemistry and the theory of evolution explain everything, from how the universe came to be to everything about human nature and the criteria to assess human flourishing. The scientific method is the only way to reliably know anything and should be the exclusive model to discover and verify truth of any sort.[8] Therefore, religion is the enemy of reason and science, which is their second grounding principle. It makes ludicrous and indefensible claims, and thus should not be accepted. But much worse, religion is a cultural evil. Religion teaches people to be unthinking, it divides people and leads to discrimination and violence, and it undermines scientific inquiry and sabotages scientific conclusions. Even in its most peaceful, moderate, and moral expressions, religion aids and abets truly heinous religious expressions, because it legitimizes the religious faith that evil fanatics depend on.[9]

What we will discover is that many of these attacks are themselves pernicious, that many of their intellectual commitments are not as rational as they think, that they lack the evidence they imagine they have and that they represent positions they themselves do not embrace in real life. New Atheism, it turns out, is an intellectual disaster and those who orbit this worldview are being taken.

The Invisible Gorilla

By the end of this book, I hope to convince you that God is like "the invisible gorilla." This image comes from an experiment called the Invisible Gorilla Test, and it has been widely used by psychologists. The test involves subjects watching a one-minute video of a basketball game. They are told to count the number of passes made by one team. At one point in the video, a human dressed as a gorilla runs onto the court and stays on camera for a full nine seconds. So the subjects view the "gorilla" that whole time, while the game around the gorilla continues on as if he isn't there. After nine seconds, the gorilla pounds his chest and runs off the court while the basketball action continues.

Fully half the subjects viewing the video do not consciously know a gorilla is in the scene. In some cases none or only one or two subjects notice and ask afterward, "Wasn't there some animal out there or something?" Most are sure there was not. Even when the video is replayed for them so that they can all now *see* the gorilla, many subjects believe the psychologist faked them out and somehow managed to slip in a gorilla video replacing the first one. That is, even with this evidence, they are sure the gorilla simply could not have been in the first showing.[10]

I think that God is like the invisible gorilla. He is there, and if you truly make yourself available to God there is evidence galore. But if your view is too focused elsewhere, if you have trained yourself not to pay attention to God, you may miss the obvious. This book, in part, is designed to help you find ways to pay attention and to demonstrate why the strategies, mistakes, and biases of New Atheists and skeptics alike impede seeing what is right before your eyes.

Chapter One

Shrill and Strange Argumentation

Shrill and Sloppy

Philosopher Bertrand Russell argues in his essay "An Outline of Intellectual Rubbish" that you can tell a great deal about the shallowness of a claim or argument by the shrillness in which it is presented.[11] We know this from our own experience. Insults are pandemic in the books of New Atheists. Here are a few samples: "Surely there must come a time when we will acknowledge the obvious: Theology is now little more than a branch of human ignorance. Indeed, it is ignorance on wings";[12] "Religious people just won't leave me alone";[13] "Believers claim not just to know [God exists] but to know everything";[14] and "The God of the Old Testament is arguably the most unpleasant character in all fiction; jealous and proud of it; a petty, unjust, unforgiving control freak; a vindictive, bloodthirsty ethnic cleanser; a misogynistic, homophobic, racist, infanticidal, genocidal, pestilential, megalomaniacal, sadomasochistic, capriciously malevolent bully."[15] This is simply not mature discourse.

Sloppy Thinking

Terry Eagleton observes, "Most critics buy their rejection of religion on the cheap,"[16] and I believe this is the case with New Atheists. We are told on the one hand that they are the cultural elite, the smartest, most creative, and most successful in society, and on the other hand that they are persecuted victims of theists. Hitchens claims that religious believers are constantly harassing him and imagines that theists want his and everybody else's destruction.[17] Harris is convinced that "people of faith want to curtail the private freedom of others."[18] And Dawkins decries systematic cultural persecution. We might ask ourselves, is this really true to our experience? Are atheists getting fired by intolerant theists? Are theists waiting to attack them for refusing to believe in God? How many murders do you recall where the victim was an atheist and killed out of some dread religious pogrom in your neighborhood or city?

Dawkins declares, "The genie of religious fanaticism is rampant in present-day America."[19] He borrowed his sole example from Harris' sole example, which is the display of the Ten Commandments in a government building.[20] Such intrusions of religion into the public square, New Atheists argue, is proof positive that religion will not remain in its own private sphere where, they also argue, it must only belong (if at all). In "A Declaration in Defense of Science and Secularism," a large number of scientists and philosophers called on our elected officials "not to permit legislation or executive action to be influenced by religious beliefs." Of course, if the religious belief is an apocalyptic one, then this certainly ought not to influence foreign policy. But the complete removal of religious values from any legislative consideration is part of the sloppy logic of New Atheists. What they are saying is that postmodern moral relativists can have a public say, nihilists can come to the table, atheistic materialists who do not believe in objective morality may influence law, and anybody else with their values can, too—just not religious believers. As for the Ten Commandments in the Alabama courthouse, what the atheists are saying is, you can have philosophers' words there, poets' words there, Freemasons' words there, words from any text or author—just not from the Bible, despite its cultural relevance. Will New Atheists have us believe that the Ten Commandments' inscription really amount to the state trying to get its citizens to embrace ancient Judaism as its favored religion? As noted in my introduction, religion has functionally been marginalized.

Another example of sloppy argumentation is the assertion by New Atheists that religious believers are less moral than the nonreligious. This would be really disturbing if it were true, and philosopher Daniel Dennett assures us that theists are now scrambling to explain this.[21] It's just a fact, we are told, that atheists are less violent or greedy than faithful people.[22] Harris announces, "One of the most pernicious effects of religion is that it tends to divorce morality from the reality of human and animal suffering."[23]

In contrast to this, I ask you to do a smell test on the claim that religions make people immoral. Consider your own city. Aren't almost all nongovernmental social services religiously originated and driven? Because I am a Catholic, I looked up the latest national data for my Church in the past year. United States Catholicism supported 561 hospitals treating 86.6 million patients; 380 health care centers treating 6.3 million patients; 1,593 specialized homes assisting 1.6 million patients; 358 residences for children filled with 29,000 patients. In addition to the many initiatives nationally, on a diocesan level, and on a parish level, Catholic Charities alone provided: social services to 3.7 million people; food services to 6.3 million people; family support, such as immigration services, counseling, etc., to 1 million people; housing services to 600,000 people; and basic needs to 1.7 million. This should surprise no one. And services by other denominations, like Lutheran Social Services, could boast comparatively.

Just for fun, I looked up the Nobel Peace Prize winners from 1980 through 2010 to find out if they were religious, agnostic, or atheistic. Recognizing sometimes multiple winners, we have thirty who were overtly actively religious and two to three who appear to be nonreligious, while two are private about their religion.[24]

It is a fact that religious people are significantly more likely to donate to charitable causes, both religious and secular.[25] According to George Gallup, "A mountain of survey data from Gallup and other survey organizations show that when educational background and other variables are held constant, persons who are 'highly spiritually committed' are far less likely to engage in antisocial behavior than those less committed. They have lower rates of crime, excessive alcohol use, and drug addiction than other groups."[26] In Gallup's article, "Dogma Bites Man: On the New and Biased Research Linking Faith and Social Ills," the dogma he refers to is the dogmatics we've seen from New Atheists.

One way to argue is just plain mockery. One of the wittiest and yet meanest expressions is Bill Maher's movie *Religulous*. Here are a couple of examples from the movie: A band of truckers gathers to pray over Maher. When they finish, he thanks them and then jokingly asks, "Hey, who took my wallet?" He's talking to the leader of the church of cannabis and asks, "So does pot hurt your short-term memory?" "Yes" is the reply. His next question: "So does pot hurt your short-term memory?" We also find that he's not duly impressed with a trucker's justification of his religious belief, and he's not ultimately impressed when an actor posing as Jesus at the Holy Land Experience theme park in Orlando explains the Trinity. But when he does talk to serious representatives, he avoids their expertise. Why? In the end, Christians come off as buffoons and Muslims like ticking time bombs. These represent his collective evidence that religion is ridiculous.

Most stunning is that their intellectual engagement challenging religion shows few to no actual representatives from the field. Dawkins, for example, uses John Hartung's critique of the Bible. In fact, he gives Hartung six pages of consideration. Here is a typical quote:

> *The Bible is a blueprint of in-group morality, complete with instructions for genocide, enslavement of out-groups, and world domination. But the Bible is not evil by virtue of its objectives or even its glorification of murder, cruelty, and rape. Many ancient works do that....But no one is selling the* Iliad *as a foundation for morality. There lies the problem. The Bible is sold, and bought, as a guide to how people should live their lives.*[27]

And who is John Hartung? A noted biblical scholar? A historian of the classical period? John Hartung is an anesthesiologist.

Weird Argumentation

Beyond these sloppy arguments, things can get more surreal. From New Atheists we learn a whole spate of things they clearly made up:

- A significant percentage of Americans would rejoice with a nuclear bomb hitting New York, for this would be the beginning of the rapture.[28]
- Religious people are trying to destroy you.[29]
- The Dalai Lama is a religious persecutor.[30]
- Islam teaches female mutilation of the clitoris.[31]
- Religion is the reason that diseases come from sex.[32]
- Christianity is responsible for the drug trade.[33]
- The reason many people believe in God is because they believe they have seen a vision of God.[34]
- Religions broadly teach that venereal disease will result from kissing.[35]
- Muslim scholars codified two categories of Muhammad's sayings under the heading "lies told for material gain" and "lies told for ideological advantage."[36]

Willful Misinterpretation

According to New Atheists, when a Christian does something evil, it is because he is a Christian, but when a Christian does something good, it is because he is a humanist, in spite of his faith. One figure will suffice to show the point. Both Hitchens and Dawkins raise up Rev. Dr. Martin Luther King, Jr., as an excellent humanist.[37] Hitchens will tell us that his civil rights crusade had nothing to do with his faith. "In no real as opposed to nominal sense, then, was he a Christian."[38] How could one fail to notice that King was an ordained Baptist minister and church pastor? Interestingly, in King's famous "Letter From a Birmingham Jail," he clearly identifies his struggle as religious, following the eighth-century prophets of the Old Testament and St. Paul in the New, and following Luther and John Bunyan in their religious quest against persecution. He refers to God sixteen times and argues that he is commanded to do his holy work of justice by God, and that God's judgment is upon the church to respond to injustice.[39]

The Straw Man

One regular way to advance the straw man in religion is to define religion or faith in a way that implies its own absurdity. For example, "faith" is regularly defined by atheists as "belief without evidence," a leap that leads "to delusion and mania."[40] Dawkins goes so far as to say that religions believe that the more your faith *defies* evidence, the more virtuous you are.[41] This makes "faith an impostor."[42] The descriptions just get odder. Harris claims that Pope John Paul II posed religious faith as that which is opposed to honest inquiry.[43] This is a striking claim, since John Paul had doctorates both in theology and philosophy—odder still, since his encyclical *Fides et Ratio* ("Faith and Reason") was promulgated to argue exactly for "the profound and indissoluble unity between the knowledge of reason and the knowledge of faith."[44]

It is also the case that many faithful people do feel free to challenge their religious authorities, so faith doesn't make one unquestioning. In fact, great religious leaders were exactly those who did challenge and question, from Jesus to Muhammad to the Buddha. Dawkins argues that the strongest faith produces absolutism and "constitutes a major reason for suggesting that religion can be a force for evil in the world"—the more religious, the more dangerous.[45]

A second form of straw man that is typical in this debate is to imagine that your theistic opponent is a fundamentalist. Here we find that the vast majority of believers apparently are more like Pat Robertson, Jerry Falwell, Osama bin Laden, and Ayatollah Ruhollah Khomeini. Dawkins claims that while many of his religious examples seem extreme, they are actually mainstream.

If you go with evangelical Christianity, why not Rev. Rick Warren, the former president of the National Association of Evangelicals? With many other leaders in the latest generation of evangelicals, Warren is particularly concerned about global warming, human rights, third-world poverty, AIDS, and many other important social issues, which he also identifies as religiously relevant. The central initiative of his Saddleback Church is P.E.A.C.E., an acronym for: **P**romote reconciliation—**E**quip servant leaders—**A**ssist the poor—**C**are for the sick—**E**ducate the next generation. Do Warren and his co-religionists seem pernicious?

Part of the fundamentalist straw man approach is to also read the Bible as if one *should* be a fundamentalist. Hitchens discovers Christianity's apparent dirty little secret: Some claims don't line up. How then, he asks, could it be the word of God?[46] "Either the Gospels are in some sense literal truth or the whole thing is essentially a fraud and an immoral one at that," he proclaims.[47]

Harris is right behind him. He wonders: If God is omniscient, why doesn't the Bible tell us about DNA, for example, or why would the Bible contradict Darwin on our origins or imagine the earth as flat?[48] Indeed, Dennett declares that "science has won and religion has lost," all because the Bible did not have evolution in it.[49]

The Christian answer is that, from the early Church on, theologians were more than aware that the Bible had various literary genres and that interpretation had to respect those genres. They also believed some texts were meant to be allegorical, some literal, and some moral. They also recognized that God's word was embedded in the culturally conditioned milieu, and they did not think this milieu had it all correct. Obviously there are Christians who approach the Bible differently, often more literally, but they would not represent mainstream Protestantism or Catholicism.

When these aggressive skeptics zero in on foolish expressions of religion, most of us religious believers wholeheartedly agree with them. So what? The human condition makes it certain there will be dysfunction in relationships, politics, social movements, institutions, sports—you name it. What New Atheists want you to believe is these odd religious examples are typical. You know they are not. Why the bad form? Why bring such shoddy sets of arguments? I believe it is because what we are dealing with is a fundamentalist atheist movement. They really don't want to see religious faith as a possibility. At least Hitchens admits, "I will always be an infidel at all times and in all places." And of the possibility to imagine "an infinitely benign and all-powerful creator, who conceived you, made you, shaped you...cares for you," he concedes, "I am incapable."[50] I will end this chapter with a telling quote by Thomas Nagel:

I am talking about...the fear of religion itself. I speak from experience, being strongly subject to this fear myself: I want atheism to be true and am made uneasy by the fact that some of the most intelligent and well-informed people I know are religious believers. It isn't just that I don't believe in God and, naturally, hope that I'm right in my belief. It's that I hope there is no God! I don't want there to be a God; I don't want the universe to look like that.[51]

Chapter Two

Background to New Atheism

Atheism in History: The Backstory

To understand modern atheism, you have to locate it historically. I am not attempting some grand detailed account of atheism as much as a thumbnail sketch to help us get our bearings. Atheism may be very old or relatively new, depending on how one interprets the evidence.[52] Some historians and philosophers have located possible expressions of it as early as the sixth century BC with the pre-Socratic philosophers Thales, Anaximander, and Anaximenes. They never called themselves atheists, but they did argue that all explanations of the material world ought to be confined to arguments and evidence that are available and open to scrutiny. So if there is a terrible storm on the sea, no appealing to Poseidon's heartburn will do.

We should also add to this ancient list the philosopher Democritus (460–370 BC), who is often regarded as the "father of materialism." Democritus argued that everything was made of atoms, the smallest reducible material. The world then operated as pure physical cause-and-effect of these atoms knocking into each other and causing ongoing movement. Their arrangement and physical quality had to do with the kind of atoms they were. Iron atoms, for example, were strong and had hooks that locked them together, water atoms were slippery, and air atoms were light and feathery in substance.

The world of Democritus was deterministic and fated. The atoms were in movement, obeyed the laws of physics, and were impersonal. Interestingly, a nuanced (but only slightly) expression of this is what is represented by New Atheists, as we shall see. Plato and Aristotle will reject the materialism of Democritus, since it proved inadequate to address the Creator as well as the metaphysical ground necessary for truth, goodness, and beauty. Still, Democritus' mechanistic framework has been adopted by the Enlightenment's understanding of scientific causality.

This literally exhausts the history of atheism until the Enlightenment and modern period. Atheism is fundamentally not part of Western culture's intellectual history until the seventeenth century. While New Atheists will tell you, "Atomism was viciously persecuted throughout Christian Europe for many centuries,"[53] the reality of the matter is that these few minor ancient philosophers were overshadowed by the Epicurians, the Stoics, and particularly by Plato and Aristotle, who hold court philosophically right through the modern period.

Michael Buckley points out that modern atheism had its curious beginning in the seventeenth century with Leonard Lessius' *On Spiritual Providence and the Eternal Soul* and Marin Mersenne's *The Impiety of the Deists, Atheists, and Libertines of This Time.* Both authors anticipated challenges to theism due to inter-Christian arguments and thus appealed to *rationes philosophicae*, that is, the science of the day.

The next benchmark in the history of atheism came with Denis Diderot and Paul d'Holbach of the eighteenth century. Both thinkers accepted Newton's assumptions that the physical world worked according to universal laws that were explainable through mathematical principles. They also embraced Descartes' belief that matter and the laws of motion worked mechanically regarding physical causes.[54] To these assumptions, they argued that the universe was not inert but dynamic, that movement was intrinsically part of matter. Descartes needed God to give the initial motion to matter, and the rest happened necessarily. Now, Diderot and d'Holbach argued that a divine first cause was unnecessary. "No one needed a god to give the first impetus to matter. It is there already; it has been there forever; motion and matter are inseparable."[55]

Welcome to the Enlightenment. The Enlightenment is a useful term to describe the ethos of modern Western culture. This ethos may have started in the late seventeenth century and it arguably represents the transition between the Renaissance's celebration of discovery and art (fifteenth through seventeenth century) and the modern period of the eighteenth century to today. The Enlightenment's cultural ethos presented a core set of values that challenged traditional institutions while vesting extraordinary faith in rationality, science, and progress. Hierarchies, rationally unsupported authority, and beliefs without evidential warrant were all suspect. This was the Age of Reason. Baggini writes, "[A]theism as an avowed doctrine is the fruit of the progression to Enlightenment values."[56]

Modern Atheism

Five key thinkers developed benchmarks in the modern expression of atheism. These would be Ludwig Feuerbach (1804–1872), Karl Marx (1818–1883), Friedrich Nietzsche (1844–1900), Sigmund Freud (1856–1939), and Jean-Paul Sartre (1905–1980). Among them, Feuerbach ranks first, and both Marx and Nietzsche identify him as an important influence. Feuerbach argued that God is a projection of humanity's most cherished values, including moral norms as well as love, compassion, freedom, and so on. In placing them on a nonexistent God, humans would then see themselves judged by God insofar as they lived these values out. While it could help people be moral, ultimately the strategy divorces humanity from its own inner life by projecting what is most noble onto a fictitious supernatural being, Feuerbach maintained. Further, this imagined projection keeps humanity in the position of a child being judged and directed by an imagined father figure. In essence, it keeps us immature.

Freud also believed that religion facilitates psychological immaturity. While it can have a certain value in keeping us moral and feeling cared for, it is ultimately a security blanket that a fully integrated psyche must cast off if one is ever to hope for full adult flourishing. Religious beliefs, Freud argued, are wish-fulfillments for the psyche. They are also used as means of coercion against antisocial instinctual drives, and at the same time recompense for citizens who properly secure those drives.

Marx famously declared that "religion is the opiate of the people." He believed that religion offered some sort of actual comfort and assurance to a people who were beaten down by the Industrial Revolution. Still, such comfort did nothing to improve cultural conditions of abject poverty and the economic slavery of the worker. Rather, religion acted as a complicit part of a corrupt society, one that promised underclass citizens that if they followed the rules that were collectively sanctioned by church, state, and capitalists, they would please God now and enjoy paradise later.

No greater modern voice for all-out atheism exists than that of Friedrich Nietzsche, whose clarion announcement that "God is dead" swept through Europe with serious impact, though mostly after his death. Nietzsche called for a complete overhaul of values and value-making. "God is dead" was not meant to simply suggest that we ought stop believing theological pronouncements and close down the churches. Nietzsche intended to deconstruct the moral and cultural ground that Europe stood upon. He found Christianity particularly disturbing because it posed weakness and humility as though virtuous. In contrast he imagined himself a prophet of a new age, the age of the *übermensch* ("great man"), who through courageous self-authorization and "will to power" constructed a dynamic self. In contrast to the slave mentality of Christianity, he called for a new kind of human race existing in power.

Compared to Nietzsche, Jean-Paul Sartre is more of a historical footnote, although an important one. Like Nietzsche, he believed that humans had the power for self-transcendence and the freedom to create themselves. Existentialism, as he defined it, means "existence precedes essence." Sartre wanted to turn our assumptions about a static human nature upside down, much like Nietzsche. It isn't, he argued, as though we have a set nature (essence) and are charged to embrace it. Rather we are radically free to create our nature by the kind of life we live. Sartre envisioned such a freedom to be utterly daunting and our responsibility then to this human project to be extraordinary. For Sartre, as for Nietzsche, atheism isn't merely about rejecting the notion that God exists. Rather, it takes seriously the necessary collapse of everything in Western culture premised on a transcendental ground, including the rejection of objective truth and objective morality. We must create these ourselves, he insisted.

There is a kind of circularity you find when you read the work of these atheists, even in the greats. They begin with the assumption that God does not exist. Everything else (world, psyche, social structures) then gets interpreted according to this principle. What is religion's real purpose? Since there is no God, then the origins of the idea *must* lie in the malfunctioning of the mind.[57] Dawkins will call it a genetic virus.[58] In short, they begin with a conclusion and then marshal an argument to support those conclusions, taking care about what evidence to look at and what to ignore, and then making sure this evidence is interpreted in light of their atheistic starting point.

The Relationship Between Science and Religion

> *There are yet people who say there is no God. But what makes me really angry is that they quote me for support for such views. But science can only be created by those who are thoroughly imbued with the aspiration toward truth and understanding. This source of feeling, however, springs from the sphere of religion....The situation may be expressed by an image: Science without religion is lame, religion without science is blind.*
>
> ALBERT EINSTEIN[59]

Many scientists, skeptics, and indeed all New Atheists claim that religion and science have been on a collision course throughout history. Religion, it has been claimed, has always been afraid of science, and every time it concedes a scientific discovery, it loses some of its own explanatory power.[60] This was Bertrand Russell's take: "[T]he clergy have fought a losing battle against science."[61] Geneticist Jerry Coyne further asserts, "The real war is between rationalism and superstition. Science is but one form of rationalism, while religion is the most common form of superstition."[62]

The Scientific Revolution and the Galileo Myth

A great pioneer in the scientific revolution in astronomy is Copernicus (1473–1543), a typical Renaissance man. He was a Catholic priest, a mathematician, classicist, jurist, diplomat, and artist. Among his many avocations was astronomy. By 1532, he had completed work on his famous book on planets orbiting the sun, *On the Revolutions of the Heavenly Spheres.* Copernicus hesitated to publish it for fear of scorn, but this was not that of the Church. Rather, he feared the scorn of scientists because he challenged basic principles of Aristotelian physics and the working assumptions of Claudius Ptolemy. Copernicus was challenging the science of the day, not the Church of the day.

When Copernicus did publish his book, he dedicated it to Pope Paul III, who was one of his many admirers. Why didn't this upset the Church? Didn't he, in fact, argue scientific claims against those of the Bible? It was now 1,200 years since Augustine taught in one of his commentaries on Genesis, *De Genesi ad litteram*, that the language of Scripture was aligned to the preconceptions and understandings of the culture it was written in. So, the limitations and distortions of that given culture are not to be taken as if fact. Augustine argued that interpretation must always accommodate itself to science. This is not to say that theological claims keep shrinking as scientific insights undermine them. Rather, Augustine realized that revelatory insights are embedded in a culturally specific and limited text. Augustine was not the first to say this, of course. Other patristic theologians, from Origen to Gregory of Nyssa, taught that the Bible ought not to be read historically in many places, even when its literary genre is itself historical.[63] Copernicus was buried with honors inside the Frombork Cathedral in his homeland of Poland. This was a site he used repeatedly for his scientific observations.

Copernicus was followed by Galileo (1564–1642). The myth of Galileo, happily perpetuated by many skeptics, is that he was a brave scientist who, because of his devotion to reason, butted heads with religion. Here's the truth of the matter: Galileo Galilei was a brilliant mathematician and astronomer. He brought his substantial intellect to Copernicus' theory along with his own improvements to the telescope, and he provided more evidence for Copernicus' hypothesis. In 1610, Galileo published *The Sidereal Messenger*, which won immediate acclaim. He went to Rome the next year and a whole coterie of Jesuit intellectuals publicly confirmed his discoveries. Pope Urban VIII rather liked him, became one of his benefactors, and even arranged for a pension for Galileo's son. In 1623, Pope Urban feted Galileo and encouraged him to publish whatever he wanted about a heliocentric universe theory. The only qualification Urban had was that he publish it as theory and not fact. This angered Galileo, since he wanted to insist that he did prove it. Actually, he hadn't. Galileo's theories would not be considered conclusive for another hundred years. His observations on sunspots, the moon, the phases of Venus, the tides, and so on provided additional support, but not conclusive evidence. As Karen Armstrong observes, "Galileo had not been able to meet his own high standards of scientific verification."[64]

Then three unfortunate things happened. First, some of Galileo's benefactors (and he had many) were implicated in Spanish political intrigues. This led to a kind of suspicion by association. Second, in 1633 Galileo published a book called *Dialogue Concerning the Two Chief World Systems,* in which the designated fool said things that Urban himself had earlier said in public. Thus, it was widely received as a direct mockery of the Pope. Finally, and unnecessarily, the miffed Pope Urban had Galileo tried for the heresy of publishing as fact what had yet to be proven. His sentence was that he be restricted to his villa in Florence. On the way home he spent half a year at the palace of one his benefactors, the archbishop of Siena. He was also given leave on a number of occasions to visit his daughters in San Matteo and allowed to continue his scientific work freely, although not on heliocentrism (not a small thing, I realize). Some of his most important publications came during this period of his life. In conclusion, the Church did indeed interfere with a scientist but had no problems with either science or his scientific discoveries. The Galileo affair is one of the New Atheists' canards.

One of the main insights we might want to get out of the Galileo affair is Galileo's understanding of the relationship between science and religion. Basically he saw none. He believed that all physical phenomena were about math and mechanics, and this was not the place for theology. Many others agreed. As his contemporary Caesar Cardinal Baronius declared, "The intention of the Holy Spirit is to teach us how one goes to heaven not how the heavens go."[65]

Johannes Kepler (1571–1630), a contemporary of Galileo, grounded his science in mathematics. What is interesting about him is that he made associations about God from mathematical and astronomical observations. In today's scientific world they seem, or ought to seem, quite strange. Kepler thought, for example, that there were five other spheres revolving around the sun, for a total of six planets in the solar system. This is what everyone believed, but for him it pointed to the glory of God. Perfect, he thought, that God is represented by the sun, with six spheres revolving around it, just like the perfect number seven. It all reflected the perfection of the Creator. He also saw the Trinity reflected as an archetype for the sun (Father), fixed stars (Son), and intermediate space (Holy Spirit).[66]

Isaac Newton (1642–1727) framed science as the universal scope of knowledge that then argued for God as the foundation for the mechanical universe. God drew up the laws and eternally grounds the universe in intelligence and power. Like Thomas Aquinas, he advocated deducing causes from effects. That is, he recognized the lawfulness of the universe, its unity, predictability, and intelligibility, and indeed its very existence, and concluded that it implied God and reflected God's glory.[67]

While surely there were, from time to time, conflicts between some scientific claims and some theological claims, these never represented large cultural tensions. Surely there were far more tensions in science itself among competing theories vying for acceptance and dominance. As for the supposed conflict between Christianity and science, one need only do a quick web search to find that there are literally hundreds of Catholic priests who were guiding figures in scientific inquiry. These would include the likes of Roger Bacon (1214–1294), forerunner of the scientific method; Nicolas Steno (1638–1686), father of geology;

Gregor Mendel (1822–1884), father of genetics; Pierre Teilhard de Chardin (1881–1955), paleontologist who discovered Peking Man; and Georges Lemaître (1894–1966), physicist and father of the Big Bang Theory.

More on Science and Religion

Physicist Ian Barbour, in his *Religion and Science*, proposes four types of possible relationships between science and religion.[68] Collectively they represent a good framework. Barbour's first type is "Conflict." Here science regards religion as an outmoded or pre-rational way of thinking. In this model, attacking religion is a truth-telling exercise that challenges believers to recognize their delusions and superstitions and become intellectually accountable. Obviously New Atheism places itself here. Fundamentalist religious believers often do as well, particularly those who reject evolution. For them, science is seen as the enemy of faith, as that godless exercise intended to undermine the religious surety they require, both to preserve their dogmas and to assure their salvation.

Barbour's second type is "Independence." Here religion and science are disciplines that are distinct from each other because they are invested in different kinds of issues. Science is about the *how* and *what* of things, while religion is about the *why* and *what does it mean* of things. Scientist Stephen Jay Gould is often quoted as a representative of the independence model. Gould writes that "the net, or magisterium, of science covers the empirical realm: what the universe is made of (fact) and why it works this way (theory). The magisterium of religion extends over questions of ultimate meaning and moral value. These two magisteria do not overlap."[69]

Barbour's third type is "Dialogue." Here the disciplines are distinct from each other and invested in different concerns, such as the *what* versus the *what does it mean* perspectives. Still, they aren't completely distinct, and they can fruitfully engage each other in ways that elevate both. Physicist John Polkinghorne endorses this position. He thinks science is constructed to raise questions that its own methodology cannot answer, but which can be addressed by philosophy and theology. Here theology works with scientific insights and makes judgments, not about the science itself but about the implications of that science with regard to transcendental issues that go beyond science's purview. The vast majority of mainstream Christians embrace this model.

Barbour's fourth type is "Integration." Here both science and religion pool their resources to create a grand narrative about the nature of the universe, a master synthesis. The great Jesuit paleontologist and theologian Pierre Teilhard de Chardin surely represents this position.

Teilhard interpreted evolution and all that it entails as part of a great cosmic design created and perpetually orchestrated by God. He interpreted Scripture, in part, by way of his understanding of science and interpreted the implications of science through the lens of his Christian faith.

Clearly, New Atheism takes on the conflict model. "All attempts to reconcile faith with science and reason are consigned to failure and ridicule," we are told by Hitchens.[70] New Atheists see the conflict model as necessary because they are committed to materialism (the only thing that exists is raw impersonal matter) and scientism (the scientific method is the only way to understand anything).[71] If these principles are correct, then religion must be false, and science and religion must be antagonistic. The conflict model is hopelessly fundamentalistic. One can be a religious fundamentalist or a scientific fundamentalist, but neither will take you very far. As Albert Einstein once observed, "Then there are the fanatical atheists whose intolerance is the same as that of the religious fanatics, and it springs from the same source.... They are creatures who cannot hear the music of the spheres."[72]

New Atheists would have us believe religion has always been

threatened by science. They also offer false choices: Science undermines religion or religion ignores science. What we have seen is that nothing of this is the case. The Church has historically been the greatest supporter of science and even tried to defend itself using the best scientific insights of the day.

Foreground of New Atheism

> *When the Cliffords tell us how sinful it is to be Christians on such 'insufficient evidence,' insufficiency is really the last thing they have in mind. For them the evidence is absolutely sufficient, only it makes the other way. They believe so completely in an anti-Christian order of the universe that there is no living option: Christianity is a dead hypothesis from the start.*
>
> WILLIAM JAMES, "THE WILL TO BELIEVE"

W.K. Clifford and William James

The warfare against religion was stoked by William King Clifford's famous essay "The Ethics of Belief" (1877).[73] In this celebrated essay he argued that science was the only path of truth and that the idea of belief without sufficient evidence was not only intellectually offensive but morally so. Clifford thought that humans have the duty to fully pursue the truth, and that believing something before one has sufficient evidence violates that duty. He also maintained that our beliefs contribute to or undermine the common good. So, what we believe and share with others affects society at large. Of course, Clifford realized that we cannot investigate and scrutinize everything. One can appeal to an authority's expertise but only if that authority is trustworthy and has no stake in the matter.

Clifford, who was a public atheist, clearly had religious claims in his sights. And they do not stand up well. Would average believers know how to scrutinize religious claims? Could they produce convincing and sufficient evidence to the skeptic? What about appeals to authority? Don't their religious leaders have a vested interest? On the surface, W. K. Clifford would seem to have the day. Who could compellingly argue that you should believe something without grounds? Bertrand Russell had us imagine a gigantic invisible celestial teapot separating the earth from the sun. Should we believe it without evidence?

William James was not one to advocate religious belief uncritically, but he took on Clifford's argument in his famous essay "The Will to Believe" (1896).[74] James was far savvier about the way humans develop beliefs. One thing that James demonstrated is that only a small fraction of what one experiences is actually taken into the conscious mind. We have filters that tend to take in information according to our experience, personalities, biases, and previous beliefs. And how we interpret and weigh evidence is also dependent on our prior beliefs. One notices and interprets experiences according to their prior assumptions and worldview. Clifford's approach imagines taking in data for evidence as both objective and complete. It is far from that. It is also the case, James shows, that different kinds of beliefs require different kinds of evidence. So, scientific evidence is not going to go far with issues such as love, justice, truth, or morality. Can we know a truth without being able to adequately articulate it? Can we have a sense of what is good before we are able to justify it by argument? Sometimes, James argued, you begin by intuition and this drives your beliefs long before evidence comes in. Science itself, he showed, often operates this way: One often begins with an intuitive confidence that something is the case, and this is only later confirmed by experimentation.

James also shows how everyone lives by faith. I, for example, believe in the periodic table of elements even though I do not have sufficient evidence, nor did my junior high school teacher.

I also trust my auto mechanic, even though I know that he has a vested interest in what he tells me. This is a Clifford no-no. Sometimes the faith you bring to a situation is actually necessary for the truth to reveal itself. So, for example, the best way a new executive is going to succeed is to have faith in the goodwill of his coworkers—this before the evidence comes in. Or suppose you have a Clifford-trained young man who's looking for a wife. He assures himself and his friends that he's no fool and that he only accepts things upon sufficient evidence. Thus, he will only date a woman who has sufficiently evidenced that she has a fascinating personality, shares his values, is intelligent, will be a good mother, is sexually compatible, and so on. Surely, these are all important. But it is also sure that our evidence-based young man will never go on a date in his life. It doesn't mean you date just anybody, nor do you believe just anything. But after some initial investigation and intuitive confirmation, faith participates in letting the evidence emerge.[75]

James' essay serves us in the most crucial way. He demonstrates that if there is a God and if there are skillful religious means of knowing God, then the skeptic's posture guarantees *not* knowing God. So, the skeptics' posture regarding how to know God is somewhat irrational. I am not saying that if you do not believe in God then you are *de facto* irrational. I'm saying that this notion that one believe something only after sufficient evidence has been garnered is a posture that is naïve, inconsistent with real life, and certainly bound to fail on this issue. It is also a principle that fails itself by definition, since it announces itself as an intellectual law without providing sufficient evidence. Clifford fails his own law.

As we shall see, there are rational, intellectually compelling reasons for religious faith. These reasons, however, do not come by way of Clifford's dogmatics but from implications of what we do in fact know of the world and ourselves.

Materialism and Scientism

Most atheists reject the idea that there are nonphysical realities. Different terms are used for this position, such as "physicalism," "naturalism," or most popularly by New Atheists, "materialism." Whatever term is applied, the rejection of nonphysical realities is the first principle that most atheists hold to. Certainly this means no supernatural realities; it also means that there is simply nothing out there except material things.[76]

The strongest version among materialists would be "eliminative materialism," which holds that even thoughts or ideas are nonexistent and that there is ultimately no meaning to anything. Most atheists believe that, though there are only physical things in the universe, this does not necessarily mean that there is nothing like thoughts, emotions, beauty, or moral values. It is simply that these come from and are wholly made up of physical material.[77] Atheists believe that positing the existence of only the material world is the best explanation, the simplest one, and the one that can be attested to by the strongest argument. In a word, God is metaphysically extravagant, an unnecessary and unprovable add-on. They will point to an adapted version of Ockham's razor. An acceptable version of this maintains that a set of phenomena is best explained by the simplest, most coherent, and most comprehensive alternative. It is the explanation that is most elegant, as scientists and philosophers say.[78]

As we will see, a wholly materialist point of view does not adequately explain a great deal of human existence, and even reality itself. The problem is that materialism is not as coherent or comprehensive as atheism imagines. So something other than nonphysical reality will not be a metaphysical add-on, but an explanatory necessity.

In the nineteenth century, T.H. Huxley (1825–1895) coined the term "scientific naturalism." By this he insisted that science must never appeal to supernatural explanations but must remain rigorously within the confines of the scientific method. Protecting the integrity of science's own methods within science is actually the teaching of the Catholic Church. Today scientific naturalism has come to represent something far beyond what Huxley meant on two scores. The first score is what we've already seen—that naturalism now refers to materialism or the belief that the only things that exist are physical. The second is an even more curious mutation of Huxley, and that is "scientism." Scientism claims that the *only* way to come to understand anything is through scientific methodology or mathematics. This reframing of things has no exact intellectual heritage, and has been criticized by philosophers of science.[79] One sees the circularity of this reasoning: Since nothing exists except parts of the physical universe, and God isn't a physical thing, then God cannot exist.

Chapter Three

Method Under a Microscope

If you only have a hammer, everything looks like a nail.

Ockham's Razor and Other Issues

As we saw earlier, New Atheists believe that positing the existence of only a material world is the best explanation, the simplest one, and the one that can be attested to by the strongest argument. In short, God is metaphysically extravagant, an unnecessary and unprovable add-on. New Atheists will point to an adapted version of Ockham's razor. Originally, Ockham's razor posited that when two explanations equally explain the evidence, one ought to choose the version with the fewest entities or causes. A co-opted version maintains that a set of phenomena is best explained by the simplest, most coherent, and most comprehensive alternative.[80] In this book, I'll assume this reframed version. But Ockham's razor also demands that your answer be sufficiently comprehensive and account for the data well. One of the many problems with New Atheism is that its explanation is not adequate, comprehensive, or often even coherent. In fact, to accept atheism's story, you're going to have to wince a number of times, accepting conclusions that are counterintuitive and assault human dignity.

One issue to address with this version of Ockham's razor is that there are typically a number of explanatory causes for something. To isolate one cause that is indeed a real cause is not necessarily to understand an issue or explain it satisfactorily. One might say that the cause of your reading these words is paper and ink. There is nothing more in front of you, and thus paper and ink exhausts the issue, because it accounts for everything. But there are obviously additional causes—ones that do not reject the paper-and-ink cause—that are not at all explanatory extravagances. These would include the arising culture of religious skepticism, my sensed moral duty to respond, my getting a sabbatical for the time to devote to deep study of the issue, a publisher, a readership, and so on. Ockham's razor doesn't say: Stop at the most reductive, most limited reference and imagine that you've adequately explained something. So, for example, we find throughout atheists' texts that "religion is man-made." Of course it is. Who would deny that human activity and the human imagination are central in the making and the ongoing operations of any religion? But does this adequately explain religion? For us, the man-made claim feels much like the paper-and-ink response. I'll grant it, but its explanatory power is utterly wanting. Consider: "We have come to the crucial stage in the history of biology, where religion itself is subject to the explanations of the natural sciences. [T]he final decisive edge enjoyed by scientific naturalism will come from its capacity to explain traditional religion, its chief competitor, as a wholly material phenomenon."[81]

Another even uglier version of the above is to dismiss the issue at the start by insisting the following: The only evidence acceptable is by scientific empiricism, and by the scientific method God cannot be assessed; therefore there is no rational basis for believing in God. Since God cannot be empirically verified, the very reference of God is meaningless. In a famous debate between Frederick Copleston and Bertrand Russell, Copleston responded to this circularity: "The proposition that metaphysical terms are meaningless seems to me to be a proposition based on an assumed philosophy. The dogmatic position is this: What will not go into my machine is nonexistent, or is meaningless."[82] Now we have some context for New Atheists to insist as an operating principle that God is a pernicious delusion.[83] On the methodological problems with science making metaphysical claims, philosopher Alvin Plantinga writes, "It is like the drunk who insisted on looking for his lost car keys only under the streetlight on the grounds that the light was better there. In fact, it would do the drunk better: It would insist that because the keys would be hard to find in the dark, they *must* be under the light."[84]

The truth is that every thinker from any discipline that I've ever read believes that scientific findings are indeed part of the explanatory story. It is just that science isn't the only explanation or sufficient explanation to cover everything. New Atheists want you to believe that if you accept evolution as a biological mechanism, then you must also believe in philosophical materialism. But why is that necessary? So asks geneticist Francis Collins, the head of the Human Genome Project. In his *The Language of God*, he describes how natural beauty, the order of nature, and the extraordinary fine-tuning of the universe point to a divine Creator. This was also the conclusion of Harvard astronomer Owen Gingerich in *God's Universe*. This point is even made by the late Stephen Jay Gould, who was an atheist: "Either half of my colleagues are enormously stupid, or else the science of Darwinism is fully compatible with conventional religious beliefs."[85]

No, say New Atheists—either/or! So we have philosopher Daniel Dennett's rhetorically charged book title *Darwin's Dangerous Idea*. As Alvin Plantinga shows, there is nothing really all that dangerous about Darwin's idea.[86] It's what Dennett does with it, that is, the philosophically unnecessary extrapolations of Darwin, that become dangerous. The problem isn't Darwin. The problem is Dennett, which I will explain in the next chapter.

Ideologically Charged "Science"

Well, who you gonna believe, me or your own eyes?

CHICO MARX IN *DUCK SOUP*

Evolutionary Psychology and Filling in the Gaps

Dawkins and Dennett rely on each other heavily in trying to explain how the human condition could be the way it is, given blind, materialistic, natural selection. They are also enthusiastic supporters of such disciplines as evolutionary psychology, evolutionary biology, and sociobiology. What all of these disciplines have in common is their various attempts to explain everything in terms of evolution, particularly how a determinist world and natural selection produce the humanity we see today. We are, in short, products of blind animality. This is a bold project indeed, with bolder claims. Take, for example, Harvard social evolutionist R.L. Trivers: "Sooner or later, political science, law, economics, psychology, psychiatry, and anthropology will all be branches of sociobiology."[87]

Evolution as the sole explanation of the human condition is particularly problematic when you look at religion, since evolutionary theory insists the only core interest an organism has is survival and replication, nothing more, nothing less. This is the thesis of Dawkins' *The Selfish Gene*, where he shows that our genes, while not conscious, act "selfishly" to preserve and reproduce themselves as their sole interest.

One might pose a number of problems to the belief that evolution is the sole explanation for all things human. Why then religion, when it wastes resources? What about altruism, which undermines reproduction and survival? What about those who give over their lives for a greater good? Easy, they maintain. We have a gullibility gene that helps prehistorical children survive;

altruism elevates our status in the tribe and ironically advances our reproductive possibilities; warriors and martyrs advance the genes of the tribe, which they share, and you're promised heaven. But, we counter, where is this "gullibility gene?" What about real compassion and selfless giving? Don't nearby enemy tribes really share our gene pool? Doesn't that leave large-scale wars (beyond your gene pool) incomprehensible? Doesn't that fail to explain actual martyrdom? Which prehistorical religion offered heaven for a warrior's death?

Couldn't we add numerous other wonderments to the list? Religions commend leaving the clan and spreading the faith outside of the clan. But this would involve losing a vigorous part of the gene pool for the good of genetic competitors. Many religions commend celibacy, monasticism, and the like, which directly undermine evolution's interests. Loving your enemy (one of the highest commands in any religion) is evolutionarily absurd. Here's the big one: Every religion I know of, along with the consensus of humanity, asserts that care for the weak, the vulnerable, the needy, and the poor, represents one of the highest virtues. The ideology of New Atheists can only find this to be an evolutionary nightmare, contrary to our nature and evolutionarily immoral to the health of our species. The weak are those whose genes should not survive and for whom care represents the squandering of our resources at the expense of our genes, indeed the future of humanity.

My point is simply this: New Atheists would have us believe that blind, natural selection in evolution has created a situation where our deepest, most profound, most meaningful intuitions about being human are not only themselves false, they also undermine our true (evolutionary) nature. And what do they offer as empirically based, scientific evidence for these conjectures? It turns out: none.

Memes

In *The Selfish Gene,* Dawkins develops an evolutionary hypothesis, which he termed "meme." Just as there are genetic replicators, he claims, there are also cultural replicators that act in the same way, only in terms of ideas. Susan Blackmore, author of *The Meme Machine,* describes them: "Memes are stories, songs, habits, skills, inventions, and ways of doing things that we copy from person to person by imitation. Human nature can be explained by evolutionary theory but only when we consider memes as well as genes."[88] A good half of Dennett's *Breaking the Spell: Religion as a Natural Phenomenon* is predicated not only on Dawkins' meme theory, but on lengthy, unsubstantiated meme conjectures. In an attempt to explain religious ideas, the meme theory holds that a religious conviction (meme) or set of interrelated convictions (memeplexes) replicate like genes through a culture.

Among the memes that religions replicate vigorously are included: "You will survive your own death," "heretics, blasphemers, and apostates should be killed," and "faith (belief without evidence) is a virtue. The more your beliefs defy the evidence the more virtuous you are."[89] I think it is obvious that human ideas are shared and adopted. If that's the New Atheists' only point, then who wouldn't agree? The problem is that they pose this theory as a scientific analogue to genetics and evolution, and in a way to undermine religion. Interestingly, they provide no evidence.

Even sympathetic scholars are starting to question memes. Biological anthropologist Robert Aunger, author of *The Electric Meme,* questions meme theory as a worthy academic inquiry. He shows, for example, that memes have no correlation with brain states, no high-fidelity replication, no independent confirmation of existence, and no way to trace their supposed origins, particularly given that many people with the same ideas had no contact with one another. "Even this brief foray into the attempts at defining memes suggests that there is a disarray at a fundamental level in the subject," he concludes.[90]

Philosopher David Bentley Hart is even less sanguine about Dennett's *Breaking the Spell: Religion as a Natural Phenomenon.*

> *In* Breaking the Spell, *Dennett advances what he takes to be the provocative thesis that religion is an entirely natural phenomenon, and claims that his thesis can be investigated by methods proper to the empirical sciences....As it happens, the case he has actually made at this point is a matter not of fact but of pure intuition, held together by tenuous strands of presupposition, utterly inadequate as an explanation of religious culture, and almost absurdly dependent on Richard Dawkins' inane concept of memes...and fortified by arguments that any attentive reader would notice are wholly circular.*[91]

Promissory Evidence

New Atheists all drive home that evidence is essential to any credible claim. That's the damnable point of religious faith, they insist: It's "belief without evidence." What we've really seen is that evidence for their own claims is rather light to nil. Philosopher of science Karl Popper has called their strategy "promissory evidence": "I'm going to tell you a story and, while I don't have any actual evidence, I *promise* it's coming sometime in the future. Trust me, the check is in the mail."[92] See how atheist Matthew Alper describes the evolution of religion:

> *Rather than allowing these fears to overwhelm and destroy us,* perhaps *nature selected those whose cognitive sensibilities compelled them to process their concept of death in an entirely new fashion.* Perhaps *after hundreds of generations of natural selection, a group of humans emerged who perceived infinity and eternity as an inextricable part of self-consciousness and self-identity.* Perhaps *a series of neurological connections emerged in our species that compelled us into perceiving ourselves as "spiritual" beings.*[93]

What scientific hypothesis has three *perhaps* clauses as its sole explanation? There is no evidence, there is no testability to the hypothesis, and there is no way to verify or disprove the claims. The so-called "scientific" deconstruction of religion is literally anti-rational. Evolutionary biologist Jerry Coyne recognizes the problem with evolutionary psychology: "Evolutionary psychology suffers from the scientific equivalent of megalomania."[94]

Overshooting Science

Science is wonderful at explaining what science is wonderful at explaining, but beyond that it tends to look for its car keys where the light is good.

JONAH GOLDBERG[95]

While New Atheists would like to convince us that scientific methodology is the cure-all for whatever ails us intellectually, many scientists recognize their own methodological limitations and the hubris of those suffering from scientism's myopia. Evolution simply has a very difficult time explaining the process of and the reason for such things as how life came about or, all the more difficult, how and why consciousness came about. Francis Collins finds the notion that evolution could be the sole interpreter of our existence utterly reductive and incredible. And he finds the arguments devised to support it painfully tortured.

How could a self-replicating information-carrying molecule assemble spontaneously from these compounds? DNA, with its phosphate-sugar backbone and intricately arranged organic bases, stacked neatly on top of one another and paired together at each rung of the twisted double helix, seems an utterly improbable molecule to have 'just happened'—especially since DNA seems to possess no intrinsic means of copying itself?[96]

How is it that atoms of hydrogen, carbon, and oxygen can

produce perceptions? What is the evolutionary advantage to consciousness? What adaptive benefits does it confer? How did unconscious life transform itself into conscious life? Even other atheists see the problem. In *The Fear of Religion*, atheist philosopher Thomas Nagel admits:

> *The reductionist project usually tries to reclaim some of the originally excluded aspects of the world, by analyzing them in physical—that is behavioral or neurophysiological—terms; but it denies reality to what cannot be so reduced. I believe the project is doomed—that conscious experience, thought, value, and so forth are not illusions, even though they cannot be identified with physical facts.*[97]

Noted atheist Stephen Jay Gould characterizes New Atheists as "Darwinian Fundamentalists."[98] While many New Atheists are scholarly thinkers and respected in many ways with regard to their subdisciplines, they show no awareness of the limits of the theory of evolution. Thus they use Darwin to try to account for anthropology, psychology, sociology, politics, culture, ethics, religion, and—even most improbably—cosmology. Further, they feel free to advance it all with no evidence.

The God Hypothesis

One of the oldest rhetorical strategies in a debate is to make the other side abandon its worldview, concede your worldview, and then argue within it. Consciously or not, New Atheists have tried to bait theistic philosophers into arguing for God on scientific terms. "The God hypothesis" is a great example of bait and switch. The strategy is to argue the philosophical question about the existence of God as though it were a scientific hypothesis. In science, a hypothesis is either an explanation for something or a conceptual framework that would bring some intelligibility to whatever one is studying. This hypothesis then is tested with replicable observations or experiments.

When New Atheists introduce the God hypothesis, they treat God like they would some thing in the universe, an object—albeit a big supernatural one—that one can experiment on. New Atheists say that the universe looks just like it would if God did not exist. In *God: The Failed Hypothesis*, Victor Stenger argues that science has disproven God by showing us that the universe looks the way it does if there were no God.[99] There is no rhyme, reason, or justice out there, but only blind, physical forces, genetic replication, and pitiless indifference.[100]

Here is the problem in a nutshell: Science, that discipline meant to study cold, material things, will necessarily be looking at the universe through the lens of its cold, material realities. If God existed, scientific research would still see materiality as materiality working like materiality. That materiality acts like materiality does not prove nor disprove God. It's the wrong kind of discourse to address this question.

So when we return to Bertrand Russell's celestial teapot we saw earlier and compare it with God, we've got a category mistake of gigantic proportions. New Atheists' assumptions, methods, and data cannot address the question of God in the way they think. They will always end up with some version of trying to refute a God that by definition wouldn't exist, that is, a quasi-physical being like other beings inside the universe. I saw this done in the debate between Plantinga and Dennett. Dennett compared the God hypothesis with a superman hypothesis. Both, in his mind, are postulated out of the blue and neither with evidence. Other atheist philosophers fall into the same trap. Philosopher Michael Scriven provides a telling analogy:

> *As we grow up, no one comes forward to* prove *that...[Santa Claus] does not exist. We just come to see that there is not the least reason to think he does exist. And so it would be entirely foolish to assert that he* does, *or believe that he does, or even think it likely that he does. Santa Claus is in just the same*

> *position as fairy godmothers, wicked witches, the devil, and ether....So the proper alternative, when there is no evidence, is not mere suspension of belief, for example, about Santa Claus, it is disbelief: It most certainly is not faith.*[101]

God is not a member of the created world. To try to delegitimize God as if he were an object in the world is an intellectual disaster. Why do they keep doing it?

Chapter Four

Sure You Want This? Implications of Atheism

Where has God gone?...We have killed him....Who gave us the sponge to wipe away the entire horizon? What did we do when we unchained the earth from its sun? Whither is it moving now?

FRIEDRICH NIETZSCHE[102]

Scientific materialism is a philosophical position, an unproved first principle that claims, without evidence, that the only existent reality is physical matter and that knowledge of anything can only be secured through the scientific method. This even includes God, which is a particularly bad, and indeed bizarre, category mistake.[103] An additional problem is the virtually absolute reliance on evolution to explain everything.[104] Dawkins writes:

> *Natural selection, the blind, unconscious, automatic process which Darwin discovered, and which we now know is the explanation for the existence and apparently purposeful form of life, has no purpose in mind. It has no mind and no mind's eye. It does not plan the future. It has no vision or foresight, no sight at all. If it can be said to play a role of watchmaker in nature, it is the blind watchmaker.*[105]

New Atheists want to put the burden of proof on believers regarding how to explain reality as we know it, particularly evil, if there is a good God. I believe this is an authentic challenge theism must address. But atheists have their own story and they are going to have to step up to the plate as well. If theists have to give a decent account of suffering and explain the differences in religions, they will have to give a decent account of their first principles. Atheists have to make their version compelling. And one of the most challenging areas for them to defend is how to understand such things as consciousness and free will in a materialistic, deterministic, impersonal world.

Scientific Materialism on Consciousness and Free Will

> *I maintain that the human mystery is incredibly demeaned by reductionism, with its claim in promissory materialism to account eventually for all the spiritual world in terms of patterns of neural activity. This belief must be classified as a superstition.*
>
> NOBEL LAUREATE JOHN ECCLES[106]

The Material Brain and Consciousness

Carl Sagan believed he described the cold hard facts about us: Brains, he said, are computers, and computers are kinds of unsophisticated brains. "Machines are just passing over an important threshold: the threshold at which, to some extent at least, they give an unbiased human being the impression of intelligence. Because of a kind of human chauvinism or anthropocentrism, many humans are reluctant to admit this possibility."[107]

Could this be true? Are we merely animated computers? Cognitive scientist and evolutionary psychologist Steven Pinker thinks so. He writes, "The computational theory of mind has quietly entrenched itself into neuroscience."[108] But what about my self? Do I have some kind of presence or being beyond this computer, something I can call my mind that is not simply the impersonal brain computer? No, say these materialists. "Man no longer has need for Spirit," declares French neuroscientist Jean-Pierre Changeux, "it is enough for him to be Neuronal Man."[109]

Francis Crick writes in his book *The Astonishing Hypothesis*, "You, your joys and your sorrows, your memories and your ambitions, your sense of personal identity and free will, are in fact no more than the behavior of the vast assembly of nerve cells and their associated molecules....You're nothing but a pack of neurons."[110]

We might want to ask ourselves then if we are even conscious. Science journalist Michael Lemonick explains the conclusions of many cognitive scientists: "Consciousness is a byproduct of the simultaneous, high-frequency firing of neurons in different parts of the brain. It's meshing of these frequencies that generates consciousness....After more than a century of looking for it [consciousness], brain researchers have long since concluded that there is no conceivable place for such a self to be located in the physical brain, and thus it simply doesn't exist."[111] "If this seems dehumanizing," neuroscientist V.S. Ramachandran announces, "you haven't seen anything yet."[112] It should be noted that everyone I quoted above is both a materialist and an atheist.

But if I do not have a self or a mind or any real consciousness, how could it be said that I have free will? How could I choose, if everything is being run by program? After all, computers have no free will. It should also not surprise us that in looking for a consciousness, they are looking for a physical thing, and this is our first clue that there may be a problem with such a conclusion.

Enter Daniel Dennett.[113] In *Consciousness Explained* and *Freedom Evolves*, Dennett tries to negotiate the problems of consciousness and free will in the context of a materialistic world, one where there is no self. Some philosophers dismiss the idea of a computational, mechanical self. They suggest that if that were really our status, we would be something akin to zombies, that is, organisms that eat, sleep, assess data, react to their environment, and so on, but have no consciousness.

Dennett recognizes the problem and responds with his theory of consciousness. This is how it goes in a laboratory: An experimenter tries over a series of many interviews to get inside the volunteer's imaginative world. With practice, one can picture the interpretive lenses of the volunteer and see how he produces the self-narratives he does. In making that discovery, one has explained the volunteer's consciousness and shared that consciousness. So consciousness is the interpretive narrative our chemical brains create as we extrapolate neuro-information. What appears to be some*one* creating a narrative turns out to be nothing but neural layering.[114]

The Material Brain and Freedom

Now we come to the tricky problem of human freedom. Can you be free as a materialist, since materialism demands that one embrace a deterministic world? Bertrand Russell faces it square on: "The first dogma which I came to disbelieve was that of free will. It seemed to me that all notions of matter were determined by the laws of dynamics and could not therefore be influenced by human wills."[115] Dennett tries to soften this blow with a version of choosing. The quick, but I think fair, version of Dennett's freedom is that we are neurologically able (as are all animals) to recognize a relevant concern in our present condition. We also have the intellectual wherewithal to anticipate a future if we act in one way or act in another. Responding in a way that is not inevitable is a kind of expression akin to freedom.

Is Dennett's position convincing? While Daniel Dennett is taken seriously by some of his academic peers on this very material, he is also highly criticized by many of them. Some have argued that Dennett really simply does not understand determinism.[116] Others show that he has at best argued for a kind of pseudo-freedom.[117] Broadly, philosophers have pointed out that in Dennett's work we find a great deal of evolutionary science but not a lot of philosophy, which is a liability for a philosopher writing about philosophy. Even sympathetic interpreters charge that Dennett ignores whole swaths of relevant philosophical discourse as if it didn't exist or matter.[118] Dennett himself admits in *Freedom Evolves* that he simply chooses to ignore many relevant philosophical issues. But he frames this as if it is an achievement:

> *I have ignored the ideas of more than a few highly regarded philosophers, sidestepping several vigorously debated controversies in my own discipline without so much as a mention....I have convinced myself—not proved—that my informal tales and observations challenge some of their enabling assumptions rendering their contests optional, however diverting to those embroiled in them.*[119]

Dennett is not alone in his reductive world, since that is the typical situation among hard-core materialists. As philosopher Timothy O'Connor observes, "Naturalists [materialists] are an educated bunch...but their intellectual diet is narrow."[120] Alvin Plantinga, one of the most influential and respected analytic philosophers in the world, finds Dennett painfully inadequate.

> *Darwin's dangerous idea, says Dennett, is that the living world was not created by God, but produced by blind, unconscious, mechanical, algorithmic processes such as natural selection, which creates "design out of chaos without the aid of Mind".... His basic ploy is just to assert (loudly and slowly, as it were) that these things must have happened providing an accompanying blizzard of scientific hypotheses and speculations...trying to show us how we can manage perfectly well without thinking there is any such thing.*[121]

Others have recognized the problem as well. Regarding mind or consciousness, philosopher B. Alan Wallace reminds us that scientists don't even know what consciousness is or how to measure it.[122] Physicist Nick Herbert agrees: "Science's biggest mystery is the nature of consciousness. It is not that we possess bad or imperfect theories of human awareness; we simply have no such theories at all."[123] Other experts in the field admit how baffling the situation is.[124]

Could it be that the scientific trouble with consciousness is that it is essentially not a material thing? As Wallace notes, "Materialist accounts appear fundamentalistically determined to preserve materialism rather than account for the data...a symptom of the metaphysical miasma induced by overexposure to scientific materialism."[125]

Implications of Materialism on Morality: New Atheists' Moral Claims

It should be perfectly obvious to all that someone can be an avowed atheist, indeed even a committed scientific materialist, and be highly moral, generous, virtuous, and so on. Therefore, it is maintained by New Atheism that being moral has nothing to do with religion *per se*, and one can derive a very fine moral framework atheistically. In fact, given that religion is such a source of moral harm according to New Atheists, one is much better off morally by being an atheist. And what is the moral good? Clearly it is happiness, Harris says.[126] Most recently Harris has published *The Moral Landscape*, a book describing how true morality is scientifically based.[127]

Some New Atheists point to Immanuel Kant, whose moral principles did not appeal to revelation. The two core Kantian principles that Dawkins highlights are two formations of Kant's categorical imperative. The first is that we are morally compelled to treat ourselves and others always and in every circumstance as an end in themselves and never merely as a means to an end. The second is Kant's imperative to truth telling. Again, one may never, under any circumstances, speak anything but what is identical to the facts of the matter.[128] New Atheists tell us these Kantian imperatives are built into us by evolution itself.[129]

What they miss is that Kant was also convinced morality

only made sense in a theistic world. For Kant, these categorical imperatives were required of us exactly because they were written into the fabric of the universe by God.[130] Kant asks: How is the categorical imperative possible? His answer is twofold. First, it is because we are free. And, since we cannot prove that we are free, we can only know it if we accept three postulates: freedom itself, the immortality of the soul, and the presence of God.[131] In Kant's own words:

> *Through the idea of the supreme good as object and final end of the pure practical reason the moral law leads to religion, that is, to the recognition of all duties as divine commands, not as sanctions, that is, as arbitrary commands of an alien will which are contingent in themselves, but as essential laws of every free will in itself, which, however, must be looked on as commands of the Supreme Being, because it is only from a morally perfect (holy and good) and at the same time all-powerful will, and consequently only through harmony with this will, that we can hope to attain the highest good, which the moral law makes it our duty to take as the object of our endeavor.*[132]

It should also be noted that Kant compares Christian morality with his philosophical morality by noting that Christian morality is hallowed, while his logical moral framework is "that of a pathetic bungler trying to interpret the former as well as he can."[133]

Even in psychologist Lawrence Kohlberg's famous moral development theory his final stage of moral development is forced to leave the sciences. Kohlberg's seventh stage is his *Spiritually Unitive Orientation.* Kohlberg recognized that the very questions fundamental to morality are philosophical and spiritual: Why be moral at all? Why embrace life? Kohlberg thought that the answers to such questions could not be solved scientifically but necessarily involve a philosophical and even contemplative approach to life.[134]

What New Atheists miss is that the implications of "the selfish gene" are that the universe is supposed to be dog-eat-dog. Didn't we already hear that Dawkins thinks compassion is a genetic misfiring?[135] How does one devise a moral vision from this? Other scientific materialists recognize the problem. Philosopher Will Provine writes, "Modern science directly implies that there are no moral or ethical laws, no absolute guiding principles for human society."[136]

What's Really Going On

Sam Harris bases his moral theory in terms of happiness. But what grounds one's sense of happiness? Donald Trump apparently thinks it has everything to do with accumulating possessions and prestige. Is that happiness? How would you know? Whom would you consult?

Of course science can help us a bit, in the sense that it can tell us about lifestyles that support such things as longevity, but this can only go so far. What about, say, Ayn Rand and her philosophy of objectivism, based on rational self-interest? Rand made a great atheist as she also claimed religions were little more than "beliefs without evidence." Rand didn't believe in positive moral rights, but rather the right to determine your own sense of value and happiness. Because of her commitment only to self-interest, she had no moral qualms about preferring her younger lover Nathaniel Branden over her husband Frank O'Connor. The only loyalty is loyalty to the self, she maintained, and any other considerations are both bound to fail and ultimately undermine others' personal responsibility. We should suppose she shouldn't have complained when Branden eventually dropped her for a younger lover (in addition to his own wife). This is the moral good, according to Rand.

Consider this: The United Nations' Universal Declaration of Human Rights begins, "Whereas recognition of the inherent dignity and of the equal and inalienable rights of all members of the human family is the foundation of freedom, justice, and peace in the world...."

We might ask, why take everyone into account? Why assume that this would be part of the natural order? "Inherent dignity" cannot be an acceptable proposition from a materialist's point of view. Isn't this an implicit recognition that it references a Creator or transcendent source of goodness, value, and truth? As philosophers Sandra Menssen and Thomas D. Sullivan note, "The prospects of finding a purely secular justification or explanation of a significant declaration of equality and inalienable rights are quite poor."[137] Philosopher Jeremy Waldron observed that contemporary literature is virtually silent about the question of how egalitarianism can be defended philosophically without a transcendent appeal.[138] The question itself is essentially ignored.

The most typical source for human rights is John Locke, but Locke's argument is based on the principle that people are capable of grasping the truth that God exists and makes moral demands. More fascinating is the discovery by Elizabeth Anscombe, a major figure in twentieth-century philosophy. Anscombe noted that as philosophers detached themselves from religious frameworks they gradually detached themselves from the belief in inalienable rights.[139] They had to.

Darwinian Fundamentalists Don't Live Their Faith (Thank God!)

Creating a moral foundation for a Darwinian fundamentalist is a harrowing project, or perhaps just an absurd one. As Dawkins points out, there are no moral foundations in a blind, materialist world. If the universe is purposeless, pitiless, indifferent, and without good and evil, as Darwinian scientistic materialists think, then exactly nothing grounds their morality. Many are on record saying this. The reason that New Atheists can be moral is that they are drawing on a religious patrimony that they don't recognize, because it is sewn into foundations of Western culture.

These include civil rights, human dignity, human equality, and a particular disposition toward those most in need. When I see New Atheists appeal to a sound moral principle, I think to myself: Where do they think they get this from? Not from evolution. New Atheists are using a set of assumptions that are theistically driven, Judeo-Christian originated, and Christian-facilitated through the last 2,000 years of European history.

Say we were to take them at their word, that there really isn't any morality in the universe and that all we have is Darwinism's sole interest in the preservation and replication of our own genes, then the following would represent the most appropriate Darwinian life principles:

- You should always and in every way treat others like means to an end and not as ends in themselves.
- Lying is appropriate if it advances your survival or procreative advantage. (Darwinian dogmatists should congratulate fertility doctors Ben Ramaley and Cecil B. Jacobson for impregnating their clients with their own sperm.)
- Any real altruism is wrong. (Mark Buchanan explains in *New Scientist* that the only reason altruistic people have not been wiped out is that Darwinism is not done yet.)[140]
- The exemplar is one who can secure the most progeny for the future.
- It would be appropriate for the human species to marginalize or perhaps even kill every member of the human race with an I.Q. under 100. This would advance our gene pool's quality better than anything we have ever done as a species. (Consider lions: A new alpha male kills

off all its competitor's cubs and quickly impregnates all the lionesses.)

- It is most appropriate that the stronger (person, race, society) oppress or at least take away the procreative possibilities of the weaker.

It may appear as though I've sunk into the rhetorical muck with New Atheists, but these claims simply follow. Darwinian materialists cannot, by their own resources, advance a moral theory that is grounded on anything beyond the dynamics of Darwinism, which they themselves have reminded us has no purpose except survival and replication.

Are You Sure You Want Real Atheism?

In *The Joyful Wisdom*, Friedrich Nietzsche tells the famous story of the "madman" who declares that God is dead. Here is part of the text:

> *Have you ever heard of the madman who...ran into the market-place calling out unceasingly: "I seek God! I seek God!"—As there were many people standing about who did not believe in God, he caused a great deal of amusement. Why! Is he lost? said one. Has he strayed away like a child?... The people cried out laughingly, all in a hubbub. The insane man jumped into their midst and transfixed them with his glances. "Where has God gone?" he called out. "I mean to tell you! We have killed him, —you and I!....How were we able to drink up the sea? Who gave us the sponge to wipe away the whole horizon? What did we do when we loosened this earth from its sun?....Do we not stray, as through infinite nothingness?...Has it not become colder? Does not night come on continually, darker and darker?....Is not the magnitude of this deed too great for us? Shall we not ourselves have to become Gods, merely to seem worthy of it?*[141]

We met Nietzsche and other atheists earlier. Here is the point of the passage: The madman actually gets what's at stake, while the bourgeois atheists around him could only laugh insipidly. As I said previously, to effectively renounce God is to deconstruct the moral and cultural ground upon which Western culture stands. You do not need to be a nihilist like Nietzsche, but you would certainly have to take seriously the full deconstruction of culture. Are New Atheists equipped? Is anyone, and by what means, and on what grounds?

New Atheists have simply not come to terms with what it would be like to drop that worldview. Do they really want Nietzsche's "will to power" as the core touchstone? Do they really want to identify and embrace Nietzsche's abhorrence with compassion for those most in need? Do they really want to deny the intrinsic value of the person and demand that such value is ascribed only insofar as that person has earned it by power? As is well known, Nietzsche was a proponent of child labor and approved eleven-hour days for children and twelve for adults. He opposed the education of workers and considered their treatment only in terms as to whether, in his own words, their "descendants also work well for our descendants."[142] In *Twilight of the Idols*, he railed against the French Revolution for its commitment to equality and justice. Considering the Nazi and Communist experimentations with creating one's own good by power, we ought to be wary of real atheism.

New Atheists would have religion simply disappear, after which we should be able to go on enjoying the same lifestyle as before, just now with less religious bother. This is exactly the kind of atheism that nauseated Nietzsche. If you're going to be an atheist, go all the way, but think about the ramifications to the bitter end. New Atheists think that we can just drop God like Santa Claus without having to witness the complete collapse of Western culture, including our sense of what is rational and moral.[143]

Chapter Five

Religion and Violence: The Big Lie

Voice or no voice, the people can always be brought to the bidding of the leaders. That is easy. All you have to do is tell them they are being attacked....

HERMANN GOERING, NAZI FOUNDER OF THE GESTAPO

Rethinking Everything: American Snapshot

"Our government makes no sense unless it is founded on a deeply felt religious faith—and I don't care what it is." When President Dwight D. Eisenhower said this in a 1954 Flag Day speech, he was widely derided. On the surface it appears a bit incoherent. Belief in belief itself is a virtue? Actually, Ike may have been on to something, wittingly or not.

Some of the most up-to-date studies on religion in America are correlated in Robert Putnam and David Campbell's *American Grace: How Religion Divides and Unites Us.*[144] The main theme of the work is to figure out why America, which is the most religious society in Western culture, is so religiously tolerant and accommodating. Among many of their findings was a high correlation between religious observance and what they call "good neighborliness."

They found that religiously observant Americans give more, volunteer more, and are more civically active. Along the lines of Ike's insight, the specific religion matters little in this regard, but the depth of engagement makes all the difference. Devout Muslims, devout Hindus, and devout Christians all look the same sociologically: solid, peaceable citizens. They also found that among those who are religiously observant, 89 percent believe that those of other religions can go to heaven. In other words, those who are devout are particularly sympathetic to religious others.

Everybody Says So

According to a British poll, the belief that religion is divisive and causes violence is now shared by 82 percent of the British public.[145] I think that this would be a widely held assumption in the United States as well. Religions are either considered *the* main cause of violence or one of the main causes, according to popular assumptions. This is imagined to be so true that some religious apologists even accept it as fact and then try to explain it, for example, moderates are not violent, only fanatics. But what if the axiom itself is terribly wrong? Of course, religious motives can and have played a part, sometimes large, sometimes small, in violence. Of course, religious differences constitute a way for people to distinguish themselves over and against one another. Of course, too, dysfunctional religion can operate in really hideous ways, just as anything dysfunctional, especially politics. It's even more complicated when one recognizes that some religious participation in violence could be for a just cause, for example, Christian ministers supporting anti-apartheid revolts in South Africa.[146]

Could it be, however, that the axiom is fundamentally false? Could this be one of New Atheism's big lies? We might want to start by asking ourselves how many U.S. wars were fought for religion. The answer is, none.[147] But must the axiom be true everywhere else? What about the Crusades? What about the Inquisition? What about the Wars of Religion that decimated

Europe in the sixteenth through seventeenth centuries? Or even today: What about Iran's Ayatollah Khomeini? What about 9/11? The evidence is imagined obvious and everywhere. While all of these are religiously motivated in some way, let us also consider:

Before the Crusades, Muslims peacefully held the Holy Land for 400 years, and Christians accepted this. What changed? More facts would include: Byzantine Emperor Alexis Komnenos appealed for assistance against the Seljuk Turks who had advanced on Constantinople; European kings wanted to reverse feudal decentralization and cut privileges of the aristocracy, thus sending lords and knights to the crusades allowed for a power vacuum; middle-class traders wanted to continue to trade with the Muslims but saw an advantage in cutting out the Byzantine middleman.

Khomeini's rise in Iran came about as a response to the brutal secularizing dictatorship of the Shah, whose ascendency came after U.S. and Britain's secret services helped overthrow a democratically elected government that wanted to nationalize its oil industry. The example of religious leaders as political leaders, like Khomeini, is a glaring exception in the history of Islam and roundly criticized by the vast majority of Muslim scholars and Muslim laypeople worldwide.

Nine/eleven was understood by the terrorists themselves as political, and part of an extremist agenda challenging Western expansionism. Many of the suicide bombers were not religious at all and were known for lifestyles violating the most basic Islamic tenets.

Did none of these have to do with religion? No, they all had something to do with it—some more, some less. It is also the case that politics and religion blur in society. The point is that these stand out as the most frequently cited and most egregious examples throughout history, and they all had more to do with politics and economics as underlying reasons. Nothing that I have said above or will address below is news to historians. What is newsworthy is that it is counter to what we assume to know—that the problem must be religion.

New Atheists' Bold and Damning Claim

> *If you tell a lie big enough and keep repeating it, people will eventually come to believe it.*
>
> Joseph Goebbels, Nazi minister of propaganda

Atheist Susan Blackmore declares quite boldly, "The history of warfare is largely a history of people killing each other for religious reasons."[148] Harris agrees that religious faith is "the most prolific source of violence in our history."[149] Dawkins claims that the problem with murderous religious fanatics is not that they have twisted their religion but rather that they have actually understood it best and are the most devout.[150]

Perhaps the most frequently cited illustration that supposedly clearly shows how religion causes violence is the collective Wars of Religion in the sixteenth and seventeenth centuries in Europe, the Thirty Years' War being the worst. Consider that the Europeans shared the same culture and history, and indeed they needed each other for trade. In spite of this, they allowed the most insignificant religious minutiae to generate hatred and violence that decimated their wealth and compromised future prosperity for a good century. That's the assumption.

The troubling problem is that little of it is based on fact. In a penetrating book on religion and violence, *The Myth of Religious Violence: Secular Ideology and the Roots of Modern Conflict*, William Cavanaugh unmasks the modern myth. With ten pages of bullet points, he gives fifty examples of major conflicts during the Wars of Religion where religion certainly could not have been involved. He points out numerous times when Protestant and Catholic peasants together revolted against Protestant and Catholic land owners, where Catholic countries were sometimes allied with Protestant princes, where the Papal states conflicted with Catholic France, where France allied itself with Muslim Turks against the Catholic emperor—the list is massive.

The Twentieth Century

> Ricky Ricardo: *Lucy's actin' crazy.*
>
> Fred Mertz: *Crazy for Lucy or crazy for ordinary people?*
>
> *I Love Lucy*

In 2004, the BBC commissioned the University of Bradford's Department of Peace Studies to conduct what they termed a "war audit" for its program What the World Thinks of God.[151] The authors describe the "oversimplifications that have crept into the media reporting the prominence that war occupies in one religion or another." They broke the religious question down variously: (1) religion as a mobilizer; (2) religious motivation and discourse by political leaders; (3) attacks on symbolic religious targets; (4) conversion goals; and (5) strong support by religious leaders.

They indeed found two candidates high in religious associations, these being the Arab Conquests (632–732) and the Crusades (1097–1291). Interestingly, they found that religion was not a motivating factor in any major war of the twentieth century, and that this was also the case in the emerging twenty-first century as well. "What many represent as religious wars have more convincing explanations as manifestations of politics, not religion," they asserted. We could also consider the death tolls of regimes that are based on atheistic principles. Here we would find something in the area of: Stalin at 25 million; Nazism at 9 million; Maoism at 35 million; Khmer Rouge at 2 million, for a grand total of 71 million. To quote the war audit: "Atheistic totalitarian states... have perpetrated more mass murder than any state dominated by a religious faith." As Tina Beattie reflects:

If we add these total death tolls of World War I (15 million) and World War II (50–55 million), and we bear in mind that many of these deaths occurred in the heart of Europe in the aftermath of the nineteenth-century triumph of science and reason over religion and superstition, we should surely be skeptical of those scientific rationalists who continue to blame religion for most of the violence in the world.[152]

We could also recall that soon after the Goddess of Reason was enthroned in the Notre Dame Cathedral in Paris in 1793, tens of thousands of religious believers were slaughtered simply for believing in God. Just a little quick math: Spanish Inquisition, more than 350 years: 3,000–5,000 persons; atheists in seventy years: 71 million persons.

How do you manage to advance atheism on the assurance that atheism is peaceable and rational and religion is violent and irrational, all the while living in a period where atheistic regimes have killed more than 70 million innocent citizens and another 70 million have died in secular wars in just this last century? The answers that New Atheists give are nothing short of bizarre.

Hitchens' main claim is that the church was somehow responsible for the 9 million innocent civilian murders committed by the Nazis. (He also believes that most Stalinists were really Christian.) Dawkins wants to blame Christianity, too, and says that one of the reasons Adolf Hitler wanted to kill all the Jews was that he was all too influenced by Martin Luther.[153] Harris advances that Nazism was really an offshoot of Christianity and therefore the Nazis were really agents of the Christian religion.[154] Another way to solve the atheist killing-machine problem is to deny that these atheists were actually really atheists. Both Dawkins and Harris argue that they were all delusional atheists.[155] Finally, Hitchens argues that these atheistic regimes acted like religions. If this is the case, then his position is really that the atheist religion really is violent, just not his denomination of it.[156]

Here is the truly rational conclusion by authors Tom Pyszczynski, Sheldon Solomon, and Jeff Greenberg in *In the Wake of 9/11: The Psychology of Terror*:

> *[T]he most horrible genocidal atrocities of the past century and, indeed, in recorded history...were all perpetrated in the name of atheistic ideologies that made no provisions for an afterlife and were sometimes directed at eliminating those who believed in an afterlife. What more compelling evidence could there be that it is misguided to point the finger of blame for this or other humanly perpetrated atrocities at religion?*[157]

Islamophobia: A Special Case of Hate

> *When the world is compelled to coin a new term to take account of the increasingly widespread bigotry, that is a sad and troubling development. Such is the case with Islamophobia.*
>
> KOFI ANNAN[158]

The problem is growing. Just a few months after 9/11, 39 percent of Americans had a negative view of Islam. In 2006 it had grown to 46 percent. How could it be growing? Have there been more horrific attacks on American soil? Who's feeding the distrust, the animosity? This is what New Atheists teach:

- The idea that Islam is a "peaceful religion hijacked by extremists" is a fantasy...because most Muslims are *utterly deranged by their faith.*[159]
- The only future devout Muslims can envisage—*as Muslims*—is one in which all infidels have been converted to Islam, subjugated, or killed.[160] Terror is part of Islam; this is the mainstream interpretation.[161]
- Islam, more than any other religion human beings have devised, has all the makings of a thoroughgoing cult of death.[162]

- The world, from the point of view of Islam, is divided into the "House of Islam" and the "House of War."[163]
- Is Islam compatible with a civil society? I believe that the answer to this question is no.[164]

The great problem with Islam, it is imagined, is that Muslims don't think like we do. They want a theocracy and won't stop without getting it. They are anti-modern ideologues, and war and suicide bombing are all they know. Is Islam associated with or sympathetic to terrorism? It turns out it has a negative correlation.[165] This and many of the following findings come from a six-year Gallup poll of hour-long face-to-face interviews with tens of thousands of Muslims in more than thirty-five predominantly Muslim countries, making it the most comprehensive study of contemporary Muslims ever done. Gallup also asked if it was justifiable to use terror on citizens. Few among the respondents thought it was justifiable on religious terms. Rather, those who did framed it in political terms, such as, "It is the only way to get America to remove its military bases." Of course, it's more complicated. Palestinian suicide bombers are often praised as martyrs, and distinguishing political from religious martyrdom is often impossible.

Religion frequently eschews violence, especially terrorism, even as our media regularly aligns them. Take the suicide bombing in the 1980s by Hezbollah, Hitchens' smoking gun in Beirut. The attackers included eight Muslim fundamentalists. But it also included three Christians and twenty-seven nonreligious Communists or socialists.[166] Indeed, a major study by Robert Pape on suicide attacks since 1980 found the following:

> *The central fact is that overwhelmingly suicide-terrorists attacks are not driven by religion as much as they are by a clear strategic objective: to compel modern democracies to withdraw military forces from the territory that terrorists view as their homeland. From Lebanon to Sri Lanka to Chechnya*

> *to Kashmir to the West Bank, every major suicide-terrorist campaign—more than 95% of all the incidents—has had as its central objective to compel a democratic state to withdraw.*[167]

Here is an interesting comparison: When Americans are asked if "bombing and other attacks intentionally aimed at civilians are *never* justified," only 46 percent agree. A full 24 percent think that aiming at innocent civilians was "sometimes" or even "often" justified. In contrast, some of the largest Muslim countries in the world responded with a much higher percentage saying that such bombing was *never* justified. This included Indonesia at 74 percent, Pakistan at 86 percent, and Iran at 80 percent. Six percent of Americans think that targeting innocent civilians is *completely justified.* But only 2 percent think so in Lebanon and Iran, and only 4 percent in Saudi Arabia.[168] Isn't the obvious conclusion that Americans are more supportive of terrorism than Muslims over the world?

To imagine Islam as a warring religion is simply false, both theologically and historically. This is not, however, to suggest that it has nothing to do with war or violence. Muhammad himself led battles, and early Islam spread through the help of early military conquest. By tradition, Islam embraces a virtually identical just war policy as the West. Violence is only acceptable when: (1) the cause is just; (2) it protects public order; (3) it would be proportionate to the injustice it addresses; (4) it is the last resort; (5) it is likely to succeed; (6) it would result in lasting peace; (7) it would never directly intend killing noncombatants; and (8) it would never include treachery or dishonor, for instance, breaking a treaty.[169]

According to Gallup's massive six-year initiative, Muslims in Muslim-dominated countries do not see the West as monolithic. They criticize and praise countries based on their policies, not culture or religion. In contrast to the myth that they are anti-modern, most Muslims admire the West for technology and democracy. Most Muslims least admire the West in terms of moral decay and a breakdown of values, which is also what most Americans least admire about their own culture. What most Muslims want from the West is to stop interfering in the internal affairs of their countries and to respect their own political rights. Their top frustration with the West is the widespread lack of respect and denigration of them as Muslims and of the religion of Islam. The majority of Muslims want a democratic society that includes general Islamic norms but is also pluralistic. They do not want a theocracy, nor do they want religious leaders having any direct role in crafting their constitution or acting as government officials.[170]

A More Penetrating Response: The Myth of Religious Violence

The myth of religious violence has a history, and it is related to how we frame violence associated with religion and violence associated with the state. Recall above that many so-called Wars of Religion were often not really religious wars at all. How did the name stick? The history of framing these and many other conflicts as religious is the history of the rise of the secular state. Regarding the question of violence, the myth of religious violence corresponds to the myth that the state does not cause war but would be the solution to the war. William Cavanaugh shows how over the last 400 years, era by era, modern states have progressively moved in this direction. By framing religion as that enterprise that is publicly irrational, divisive, and a cause for violence, the state can demand loyalty by characterizing itself as that which unites by overcoming the irrational because it is secular. Cavanagh writes, "The myth of religious violence reinforces a reassuring dichotomy between religious violence—which is absolutist, divisive, and irrational—and secular violence, which is modest, unitive, and rational."[171]

Now we have reason for creating war. We are halting violence by means of war. Saving the Middle East by making war with it amounts to secularism. "Secularism," Hitchens says, "is not just a smug attitude. It is a possible way of democratic and pluralistic life that only becomes thinkable after several wars and revolutions had ruthlessly smashed the hold of the clergy on the state."[172] For Harris, since religious people hold religious beliefs, they are *de facto* irrational. Thus, there's no sense trying to reason with irrational people. They can only be dealt with by force. The myth of religious violence is his singular justification for the use of violence. Bizarrely, Sam Harris advocates first-strike nuclear destruction against any Islamic-controlled country that possesses nuclear weapons, admittedly murdering "tens of millions of innocent civilians in a single day."[173] Cavanaugh concludes his masterful study in part by the following:

> *The myth of religious violence is also useful, therefore, for justifying secular violence against religious actors; their irrational violence must be met with rational violence....If they are not sufficiently rational to be open to persuasion [cooperating with our foreign policy interests] we must regrettably bomb them into the higher rationality.*[174]

Chapter Six

Rethinking Religion

Rationalized interpretation of religion has resulted in two distinctly modern phenomena: fundamentalism and atheism.

KAREN ARMSTRONG[175]

Not Christian or Jew or Muslim, not Hindu, Buddhist, Sufi, or Zen.

Not any religion or cultural system....My place is the placeless, a trace of the traceless. I belong to the Beloved.

RUMI[176]

One of the challenges that religious skeptics of all kinds hold is that there is a plethora of religions, each with its assortment of strange, virtually incomprehensible claims that themselves compete with one another. So, even if God did exist and has revealed truths to humans, there is still no intelligible way to know which of these competing sets of claims comes from God. Let's make matters even more precarious, they charge. According to these religions, if you get the wrong answer, you experience eternal damnation. This religious situation was satirized in a *South Park* episode, where on the last day all souls are gathered around the gates of heaven. Saint Peter comes out and says something like, "Thank you all for coming. We will now open the gates for God's true children to enter and the rest of you will have to enter hell. It turns out God is Mormon. That's right, the correct answer is Mormon."

What Religions Really Think: Religion and Religious Claims

I think these charges are misleading. I vigorously challenge the assumption that religions are primarily about making religious claims, and I challenge the assumption that many of these claims compete with other religious claims head to head in the decisive manner assumed. Broadly speaking, religion is more about right action than right belief. Muslims, Jews, Hindus, Buddhists, and every indigenous tradition I've studied all place more weight on authentic spiritual living than maintaining accurate truth claims. The truth about religion is discovered by engagement. Karen Armstrong makes an interesting point:

> *You cannot learn to dance, paint, or cook by pursuing texts or recipes. There are some things that can only be learned by constant, dedicated practice....Religion is a practical discipline that teaches us to discover new capacities of mind and heart. People who acquired this knack discovered a transcendent dimension of life that was not simply in external reality "out there" but was identical with the deepest level of their being.*[177]

Religions do, of course, make truth claims. For instance: God is Trinity, *atman* is *Brahman*, the Quran is inerrant. Yet religious claims have a context, that is, the realm of relationship with the divine, the inner self, and the world; it is the realm of beauty and transcendent meaning. In his penetrating book *Religion*, philosopher and historian of ideas Leszek Kolakowski writes, "Religion is not a set of propositions, it is the realm of worship wherein understanding, knowledge, the feeling of participation in the ultimate reality...and moral commitment appear as a single act."[178]

Healthy, authentic religious expressions are not anti-intellectual, nor are they anti-science. What they are, instead, is a more robust expression of the human experience and intellect. Consider the following scenario: A colleague of mine just got a new, young priest assigned to his parish. I asked him how he liked this new minister. "I'm not crazy about him," he replied. It turns out that this young priest was kind, hard working, and attentive to his pastoral duties. That wasn't the problem. "It's his preaching," my colleague said. "He talks a good game, and there's nothing really that I would disagree with. The problem is that guy just hasn't bled enough to say what he says." What an interesting insight. His dissatisfaction reveals that preaching isn't fundamentally about communicating truth claims as if scientific claims. Preaching is about witnessing a fully engaged faith life, about communicating the dynamics of human existence in the context of a life with God, about courage and humility, about authenticity and interior depth. This young priest overplayed his inexperienced hand.

Finally, one ought to be careful imagining contradictions among religions' beliefs when there is no essential contradiction. Obviously, the Christian claims about the triune nature of God and that Jesus Christ has both a human and divine nature are not shared by Jews and Muslims. Obviously, Muslim claims about the eternal Quran are not shared by Jews and Christians. And these are important. But one ought not to exaggerate those differences. Fundamentally, Western religions believe that we are created in God's image and likeness for union with God both now and fully in eternity, and that we will be judged on the degree that through God's grace we have pursued the true and the good and lived them in our lives by service and love to others. Buddhism, Jainism, and Hinduism all assume the quality of rebirth is predicated on spiritual development and moral living, and liberation is imagined to be radical freedom. Indeed we could even leave these specific alignments of religions and see some universal agreements. So while Western traditions believe in some kind of union with God, many Native American traditions also believe in a spiritualized paradise, and Hindus proclaim a union of self and God (atman and Brahman). This is not to collapse these religions and their distinctions, but it is to stay the shrill voice that cries out that it is a metaphysical nightmare of mutual religious contradictions.

How Religions See One Another

The way many skeptics frame religions is that they simply misrepresent what other religions actually believe about each other. Harris declares, "As long as a Christian believes that only his baptized brethren will be saved on the Day of Judgment, he cannot possibly respect the beliefs of others, for he knows that the flames of hell have been stoked by these very ideas and await their adherents even now."[179] We are also told that "intolerance is thus intrinsic to every faith, and respect for other faiths, or the views of unbelievers, is not the attitude that God endorses."[180] This is an example of the straw man argument, one in which after showing how absurd it is, he can apparently claim victory. Still the victory is pretty hollow when we find out he's talking about a decided minority.

Let's consider Roman Catholicism as a test case. Catholicism asserts that all are called to salvation by God and that God will ensure that this is a real possibility. In the Second Vatican Council's Dogmatic Constitution on the Church, *(Lumen Gentium* 16), we find, without intending to be an exhaustive list, that...

> *those who have not yet received the Gospel are related in various ways to the people of God. In the first place we must recall the people to whom the testament and the promises were given and from whom Christ was born according to the flesh. On account of their fathers this people remains most dear to God, for God does not repent of the gifts He makes nor of the calls He issues. But the plan of salvation also includes those who acknowledge the Creator. In the first place amongst these there are the Muslims, who, professing*

to hold the faith of Abraham, along with us adore the one and merciful God, who on the last day will judge mankind. Nor is God far distant from those who in shadows and images seek the unknown God, for it is He who gives to all men life and breath and all things, and as Saviour wills that all men be saved. Those also can attain to salvation who through no fault of their own do not know the Gospel of Christ or His Church, yet sincerely seek God and moved by grace strive by their deeds to do His will as it is known to them through the dictates of conscience. Nor does Divine Providence deny the helps necessary for salvation to those who, without blame on their part, have not yet arrived at an explicit knowledge of God and with His grace strive to live a good life. Whatever good or truth is found amongst them is looked upon by the Church as a preparation for the Gospel.

According to Roman Catholicism, even atheists can potentially go to heaven. The presumption is, of course, that they really are striving to be open to the true and the good. Their cooperation with the secret working of grace is what they are being judged by, not whether they have the right propositional claims. Attention to one's conscience is how religious believers are going to be judged as well. This is called the "inclusivist" position, and represents Catholicism, the Orthodox communion, the Anglican communion, and mainstream Christian churches. There is also the "pluralist" position among some Christians. These Christians refuse to name Christianity as the singular normative religious revelation. They argue that God transcends comprehension and thus all doctrines, and that no one religious paradigm can embrace all metaphysical truths from all angles. While no denomination has signed off on this perspective, there are highly respected voices in the theological world that do.

Finally, there is the "exclusivist" position, and this is the one that many skeptics assume is common. Here, if you are not Christian, you will be damned for it. I share the New Atheists' challenge of this view, which some (but not most) Evangelical Christians still embrace. But I also challenge New Atheists to find many real contemporary examples of it in the theological community or even among major Evangelical leaders. Harvard professor Francis X. Clooney, the world's leading expert in comparative theology, reports that there are virtually no theologians who are bona fide exclusivists.[181] Most Evangelicals follow their mission without presuming to know the divine mind on such things. This is the position of Billy Graham.

What's particularly interesting about this conversation is that Christianity is particularly restrictive in its understanding compared with other religions. Jews, for example, believe that their job is to be a light to the nations and witness Torah. They don't think that God wants everyone to be Jewish, and heaven forbid you imagine you'd have to be so to get saved. Muslims take a Christian inclusivist tack. They believe anyone can be saved and that you certainly do not have to be a Muslim. Most Hindus and Buddhists believe that final liberation will come when one realizes by experience and transformation central truths that are best facilitated by their own specific religion. Still, because they believe that every person will necessarily go through millions of lifetimes, they think one might very well be better off in another religion now. Many Hindus think Jesus is an incarnation of Vishnu and Westerners should be Christian, and many Buddhists, such as the Dalai Lama, think that the Abrahamic religions represent the Dharma in the West during this current epoch.

The Moral Life

Many atheists and skeptics discuss the Bible as if it ought to be interpreted literally and as if the historical conditions from which it emerged are inconsequential. They also often imagine that the Bible is exclusively about moral teachings. Dawkins poses it as a compendium of moral rules and then shows how the rules are twisted or the moral role models are hopelessly pathological. He thus concludes that the Bible should never be the source for modern morality.[182] Harris concurs, and shows us how, if you took the Bible seriously, you would be stoning your children for disrespecting their parents.[183]

The moral complexity of religious texts is no news. If you read the Hindu Mahabharata you will discover a complex narrative that is both ribald in many places and profound in many other places. Sometimes the vulgar and the spiritually extraordinary are enmeshed in the narrative. One of my assignments in my freshmen Theology 101 course is to argue whether David was a hero. Here we find a warrior, a poet, a man who can be extraordinarily courageous and virtuous, as well as an adulterer, murderer, briber, and so on. My students see that even coming to a cogent answer for the assignment includes considering the cultural rules at the time. They also see how power can corrupt the heart. They see something of the dynamics of sin, forgiveness, and faithfulness. Some students are a bit shocked at the material, but few—if any—are ultimately scandalized. We find a rich text that speaks wisdom about the human condition and God's engagement with it.

When New Atheists see the antiquated laws in Leviticus as if representative of God's eternal moral laws for Jews and Christians, we see a document in the historical context of Semitic neighbors who sacrificed children to their gods and whose fertility rites included sex with temple prostitutes. If you were to look for large themes, what you see are not antiquated rules about stoning violators but dominant principles such as the prophetic association of true worship with social justice.

Jesus' Sermon on the Mount serves as a great illustration, even as skeptics imagine it insipid.[184] The sermon works as an illuminating example. It begins with the Beatitudes:

- Blessed are the poor in spirit, for theirs is the kingdom of heaven.
- Blessed are those who mourn, for they will be comforted.
- Blessed are the meek, for they will inherit the earth.
- Blessed are those who hunger and thirst for righteousness, for they will be filled.
- Blessed are the merciful, for they will receive mercy.
- Blessed are the pure of heart, for they will see God.
- Blessed are the peacemakers, for they will be called children of God.
- Blessed are those who are persecuted for righteousness' sake, for theirs is the kingdom of heaven.[185]

Jesus goes on in his sermon to exhort them to interior purity and spiritual transformation: Instead of merely avoiding murder, remove the toxin of anger; instead of merely avoiding adultery, free yourself from the imprisonment of lust; instead of merely honoring oaths, make your whole life truthful and transparent; love your enemies; do good to those who cannot return the good back; give without self-congratulation or public fanfare; instead of hoarding money, store up spiritual treasure; free yourself from obsessive fears and trust God's love; stop judging others; know of God's care for you; what you want for yourself, offer for others; and be a doer of God's will, not just a talker.

Of course, the Sermon on the Mount cannot give us specific moral practices. It cannot tell us, for instance, whether World War II was a just war. The challenge to love one's enemies and be nonjudgmental does not suggest felons ought not to be held accountable. But such considerations do not mean that the Sermon on the Mount has nothing to do with morality. It teaches us that even those who would do us harm have the same intrinsic dignity as we do. It moves the heart to value restorative justice over pure retribution. It is a vision or perhaps a spiritual and moral lens through which we see the world. It provides a posture that guides moral knowing.

Consider the 2006 Amish school shooting in Nickel Mines, Pennsylvania. The gunman, Charles Roberts, shot ten girls, killing five, before committing suicide in the schoolhouse. The Amish community, including the victims' family members, expressed forgiveness for the clearly sick murderer and then reached out to help heal the perpetrator's own family members. One Amish man held Roberts' weeping father in his arms for an hour to comfort him. Finally, about thirty members of the Amish community went to Roberts' funeral, and the community then set up a charitable fund for the family of the shooter. All this healing was made possible by people who allowed themselves to be grounded in Jesus' vision. This is insipid?

From the Bible we see that all are made in the image and likeness of God. Materialists say that we have no intrinsic value. You don't even have to go the distance with Nietzsche, who thought human value had to be earned through power. You could merely listen to Peter Singer, Princeton University's foremost utilitarian philosopher and atheist. Singer argues that small children and the frail elderly are simply less valuable than healthy adults and thus warrant less moral consideration—even the right to life.[186] Can you kill a Down Syndrome-born child? The Judeo-Christian vision sees all human beings as inherently precious. Or do you consider them "deformed or idiot children" (Hitchens' actual words)?[187]

Moral norms do not just come out of nowhere. They are derived from a vision. The moral vision I receive from my Church includes: The core truth of the universe is love; you are utterly loved by God; every person is intrinsically important; there is truth in the universe, and you were made to seek it, find it, and understand it; your truth is God's truth, and you find your truth as you find God; using others merely as means to an end violates them, you, and God's law; your flourishing depends on aligning yourself to values that you did not create, but which you recognize are already there. By submitting to them you paradoxically experience your personal power and freedom.

A Religious Questioning of Atheism

Recalling Ockham's razor, I find atheism incomprehensible, not because I refuse to listen to atheism's challenges, but because atheism fails to deal with so much. So while a simplistic answer to the question of how the human species came to exist might be evolution, it turns out to be a very poor explanation in and of itself because it has to ignore and skew so much. Let us just briefly recall the New Atheists' explanatory version:

> *Natural selection, the blind, unconscious, automatic process which Darwin discovered, and which we now know is the explanation for the existence and apparently purposeful form of life, has no purpose in mind. It has no mind and no mind's eye. It does not plan the future. It has no vision, or foresight, no sight at all. If it can be said to play a role of watchmaker in nature, it is the blind watchmaker.*[188]

Darwin's dangerous idea, Dennett teaches, is that the world is produced by blind, unconscious, mechanical processes. As Dawkins assures us, "Life *is* empty."[189] If this is what they really believe, then their moral vision would have to include: There is no actual thing as love; you were not created by or for anything of real value, because there is no real value; your genes are important, but only to you, and propagating them is the prime directive of your life; there is no moral, spiritual, or purposeful truth about you or the universe; you create your own illusion of truth and then you exist in it; you are not free to self-authorize your life; and your life really is empty—face this.

Most religions hold for some kind of conclusion to history in a full transcendental existence. We are convinced that who we are and what we do is not merely a testing ground for a ticket into that new existence. Rather, it is already a participation in it. Catholicism teaches what I think the vast majority of Christians, Jews, and Muslims believe:

> *Far from diminishing our concern to develop this earth, the expectancy of a new earth should spur us on, for it is here that the body of a new human family grows, foreshadowing in some way the age which is to come. That is why...such progress is of vital concern to the kingdom of God, insofar as it can contribute to the better ordering of human society.*[190]

Theists find materialism utterly incapable of addressing the breadth of human life and experience. Particularly, it eclipses the inner life, and everything humans simply know to be most valuable about being human.[191] Theists also find the atheistic explanatory project utterly illogical. We ask, why is the universe intelligible? Why do you even ask questions about who we are and what we mean? If the universe is not grounded in truth and intelligibility, if it is blind, random, and meaningless as New Atheists have assured us, then what makes the category of intelligibility intelligible? What I'm getting at is we seem to be made not just for procreation in a blind, aimless world. We seem to be made to make sense of things. We religious believers think that we have a justified reason that something is grounded in truth because we believe the universe is grounded in Truth. We call that God. Atheists provide no good reason whatsoever.

The strictly evolutionary story ironically undermines the atheists' claim, while an evolutionary explanation with a divine grounding explains a great deal. The atheistic, materialistic, evolutionary account is the story of human development not aligned to the truth, but to survival. As Patricia Churchland puts it, "The principle chore of brains is to get the body parts where they should be in order that the organism may survive....A fancier style of representing the world is advantageous so long as it...enhances the organism's chance for survival. Truth, whatever that is, takes the hindmost."[192]

A materialist account cannot explain the ability to know truth as such, but a theistic account can. That is, the world is intelligible because it is grounded in transcendental intelligibility, and we have the capacity to assess the truth because we have a consciousness that extends beyond mere chemistry along neural pathways. What we have is intrinsically associated to that divine ground.

The same can be said about morality. Here is an illustration of a purely materialist, evolutionary assessment about morality by Dawkins: "The universe we observe has precisely the properties we should expect if there is, at bottom, no design, no purpose, no evil, and no good, nothing but blind, pitiless indifference."[193] At face value, materialists ought to praise lying if it supports procreation, support eugenics, and always use others as means to your own end. These are activities utterly aligned, but only aligned, to evolution's interests.

I wonder: If there is no objective good or morality, how can they be morally outraged by perceived immorality of religion or anything else? We theists shake our heads. If materialism is right and there is no objective morality, then how can we even have a discussion about morality? What perspective can atheists draw on? And wouldn't that perspective be amoral? On the other hand, if like religious people you believe there is something objective about morality, because the created world is transcendentally grounded in it, and if you believe that you have something to do with that transcendental ground, then you can start trusting your conscience. Are these principles from a materialist point of view really true?

- Morality is devoid of truth and utterly subjective.
- People have no intrinsic value.

- Awe and wonder are merely chemical.
- Beauty does not really exist.
- You cannot self-authorize your life in any way that is authentically free.

I argue that New Atheists and all materialists do not really take seriously what they claim to believe. The implications of what they claim would be to deny truth, value, beauty, meaning, goodness, freedom, a robust consciousness, and so on. But they live as though these things are real. Do they not understand the implications of their position? Atheists and theists both implicitly live in a theistic world, a world transcendentally grounded. The religious account is compelling, one that takes Ockham's razor seriously. The atheistic account fails Ockham's razor at every turn.

Chapter Seven

Religious Problems: The Big-Ticket Items

Revelation

Sam Harris articulates what most people would casually sign off on unless pushed: "Most of the people of this world believe that the Creator of the universe has written a book. There are many such books, each making an exclusive claim to its infallibility."[194] Some forms of Hinduism believe this about the Vedas, and Islam believes this about the Quran. So Harris hasn't exactly led us astray in this claim.

But there are two problems with the way he has framed it. The first is that many religions do not believe this as presented or function as if it were the case. The second problem is that these exclusive claims may be to the primacy of the text, but they are not necessarily exclusive in the sense of denying the divine inspiration of other texts. I personally don't know of anyone who thinks other religious traditions have no inspiration or truth. Interestingly, Pope John Paul II convened a day of prayer with religious leaders from the world in Assisi, Italy, in 1987. In a lecture on that interreligious experience, he stated, "There are undeniably differences [in religions] that reflect the genius and spiritual 'riches' that God has given to the peoples."[195]

Many skeptics imagine revelation very differently from the way I, my colleagues, or even the members of my Church see it. They imagine a golden typewriter and God as dictating to the scribe. So, if it's really revelation, then it would be inerrant and show the intelligence of God who knows all about evolution, the Big Bang, the real length of the Earth's existence, and so on. Astronomer Carl Sagan went so far as to wonder why God didn't put the Ten Commandments on the moon, since this would prove God's revelatory activity.[196]

Since the early Church, it has been assumed that the biblical text reflected the cultural situation from which it came. So there's going to be no metaphorical golden typewriter, regardless of your theology of revelation. Religions widely believe that when God reveals himself, he does so through the psychological, cultural, sociological, and theological framework of the time. Thus, quantum theory in the Book of Genesis would make no sense to ancient Jews, even if God worked that way. Further, religions widely believe that God reveals himself through the subjectivity of the one experiencing the inspiration. That is, how that person thinks and experiences the world is reflected in the text.

The Catholic Church teaches that the font of revelation has two expressions that mutually interpret each other: Scripture and Tradition. Here Tradition refers to the living experience of the faith, from the Church at prayer to ethical intuitions, Church leadership, the spiritual lives of the community members (*sensus fidelium*), and so on. It was from the living experience of the faith that the Church chose those scriptural texts that it believed represented the authentic Tradition. The Tradition and the Scriptures are always in dialogue, and as the experience of the Church asks different questions in every era, the text becomes the Tradition's dialogue partner.

Other Christian communities would not exactly frame the issue in the same way, but they act essentially in the same manner. Sam Harris claims that "faith hasn't evolved."[197] This can only come from someone who knows absolutely no theology or religious history.

The Problem of Evil

> *If it turns out that there is a God, I don't think he's evil. I think the worst you can say about him is that basically he's an underachiever.*
>
> Woody Allen from *Love and Death*

> *How we squander our hours of pain.*
>
> Rainer Maria Rilke, *Tenth Duino Elegy*

For many sincere skeptics, overwhelming examples of pain and suffering undermine traditional belief in God. If God is both all-powerful and wholly good, God would have created a world without such pain. This is called the "theodicy" problem. One of the most interesting rejoinders I have to the atheists' problem of evil is that they pose the challenge from a theistic point of view. The fact that atheism considers this a real problem means that the questioner is grounded in moral intuitions that demand a coherent response. But if the sole explanation of who we are is evolution—that which depends on death, destruction, and violence against the weak—why would the world of violence be considered wrong or unjust? Plantinga argued that "a secular way of looking at the world has no place for genuine moral obligation of any sort....Accordingly, if you think there really is such a thing as horrifying wickedness (...and not just an illusion of some sort), then you have a powerful...argument [for God]."[198] C.S. Lewis had the same observation in *Mere Christianity* and it led him to believe in God:

> *My argument against God was that the universe seemed so cruel and unjust. But how had I got this idea of "just" and "unjust"?...What was I comparing this universe with when I called it unjust?...Of course, I could have given up my idea of justice by saying it was nothing but a private idea of my own. But if I did that, then my argument against God collapsed too—for the argument depended on saying that the world was really unjust, not simply that it did not happen to please my private fantasies....Consequently atheism turns out to be too simple.*[199]

One answer to the problem of suffering is simply that we are part of the created universe. Being a creature necessarily involves being fragile. Serious religious thinkers do not imagine a perfect world, as if the problem is our inability to see it. Actually, many imagine the opposite. Most, if not all, religions proclaim a world that corresponds to the harshness of life. We do not see ourselves separate from the created universe with its laws of entropy (everything breaks up) or from evolution with its laws of survival at the cost of great suffering and hardship. So, to imagine that the world and human existence should be other than this is to imagine not a created world but a platonic world of eternal forms, one untouched by physical reality. It's what philosopher Richard Swinburne calls a "toy world."[200]

An additional response is that much of our suffering, indeed all moral evil as well as our relationship to physical evil, is due to sin. Sin has to be a real possibility if we are to have freedom, real moral self-authorization, and accountability. Authentic religions, all of them, confront the obvious reality of sin and the responsibility humans have for it. Thus, a religious believer finds something in the theodicy challenge a bit wrongly placed. On the last day, instead of demanding of God an answer to human suffering, God will be demanding an account of us!

Is suffering really pointless? Consider raising children who are overprotected from pain. They end up weak, overly sensitive, spoiled adults. Suffering strains and separates aspects of our personality. Embracing and addressing suffering is the necessary condition for restoring ourselves in a whole new way. Remember my earlier example of a young priest who did everything seemingly right. The criticism from my colleague was that "he hadn't bled enough." Philosophers, psychologists, and literary giants have long reported and empirically verified that positive changes come from adversity and that some of those changes literally require adversity. Suffering brings opportunities for courage, sympathy, and patience. It challenges us to engage in healing, in generosity. It is the context for our expressing our free will and helps us create the kind of persons we are. This is my experience, and I trust yours, too. In describing raising an autistic child, Clara Claiborne Park notes at the end of her sensitive memoire *The Siege*:

> *So then, this experience we did not choose, which we would have given anything to avoid, has made us different, has made us better. Through it we have learned the lesson that no one studies willingly, the hard, slow lesson of Sophocles and Shakespeare—that one grows by suffering....If today I were given the choice to accept the experience with everything that it entails, or to refuse the bitter largesse, I would have to stretch out my hands—because out of it has come, for all of us, an unimagined life. And I will not change the last word of the story. It is still love.*[201]

I believe I have offered some compelling ways to consider suffering that do not undermine theism or religion, but rather support religious intuitions. In fact, religions offer one more. Religions hold that suffering is not the final word in human existence, but rather union with God is. Union with God is the natural and supernatural fruition of a life of faith for a human being made for union with God. In short, suffering is not the last word. Here is how Dostoyevsky and Lewis framed the same conviction:[202]

I believe like a child that suffering will be healed and made up for, that all the humiliating absurdity of human contradictions will vanish like a pitiful mirage, like the despicable fabrication of the impotent and infinitely small Euclidean mind of man, that in the world's finale, at the moment of eternal harmony, something so precious will come to pass that it will suffice for all hearts, for the comforting of all resentments, for the atonement of all the crimes of humanity, of all the blood that they've shed; that will make it not only possible to forgive but to justify all that has happened.

FYODOR DOSTOYEVSKY, *THE BROTHERS KARAMAZOV*

They say of some temporal suffering, "No future bliss can make up for it," not knowing that Heaven, once attained, will work backwards and turn even that agony into a glory.

C.S. LEWIS, *THE GREAT DIVORCE*

Hell

One of the most vexing challenges that atheists (and others) pose to Western theists is the doctrine of damnation. You may recall that Jews, Muslims, and Christians widely believe that God desires and makes possible the salvation of every soul. So, the charge that God is waiting to send everyone who doesn't believe in my religion into hell is simply not how Western religions operate (nor Hinduism, Buddhism, Jainism, Daoism, Confucianism, Shinto, etc.).

But we shouldn't dismiss the problem as if it then is no problem. We might consider it like this: How could an all-loving God send someone into an absolute punishment, with all the emptiness, horror, and pain, that this would involve for eternity? While some important theologians from Christianity like Gregory of Nyssa and the modern great Hans Urs von Balthasar, as well as those in Islam and Judaism, believe in absolute universal salvation, mainstream Christianity, Islam, and some versions of Judaism assert a heaven and a hell as real afterlife possibilities.

Czeslaw Milosz, the Nobel Prize-winning poet, wrote an essay titled "The Discreet Charms of Nihilism." In contrast to Marx, who imagined the promise of an afterlife as part of "the opiate of the people," and in light of Nietzsche's frightening nihilism, he challenged, "And now we are witnessing a transformation. The true opium of the people is a belief in nothingness after death—the huge solace of thinking that our betrayals, greed, cowardice, murders are not going to be judged [but] all religions recognize that our deeds are imperishable."[203]

Part of a typical way that theists who believe in heaven and hell frame the issue is one of love and freedom. If by its very nature love cannot be forced and if we are really free, then it must be possible to reject God, and God must respect this. It is also the case that, in contrast to most New Atheists, theists believe that human beings really do self-authorize their lives. We really are free, and robustly so. And this makes us accountable for the person we make ourselves to be. Obviously our freedom is limited by our circumstances, life experience, natural gifts or lack thereof, even what is called moral luck. Obviously then theists widely believe that only God knows the soul, knows its suffering, and knows how it has or has not responded to what it has been given.

Jews, Christians, and Muslims dedicate our dearly departed to the mercy of God, not because mercy is in conflict with justice, but because compassion and love represent the foundations for God's justice to be expressed. But they also insist that human beings create a fundamental direction in their lives. No one dies with a perfectly pure heart. But some have fundamentally directed their lives to the good and the true, and heaven is the fruition of that exercise of freedom. Further, others have fundamentally directed their lives to rejecting the good and the true, and hell is the result of that exercise of freedom. It is a question of this one precious life and how we have authorized it in our freedom.

Miracles in an Age of Science

One of the great texts against religions, and certainly an important part of the atheistic canon, is David Hume's essay "Of Miracles," from his book *An Inquiry Concerning Human Understanding.*[204] Hume defines miracles as a violation of the laws of nature, and most skeptics sign off on this as a definition. They wouldn't be alone. Most believers imagine the same thing: A miracle is exactly something that doesn't happen in accord with the laws of nature. That's what makes it a miracle. Here are some of the problems with miracles, as Hume sees it: Witnesses are often compromised by their enthusiasm and imagination; they offer no evidence; there are few witnesses; it represents a prescientific imagination; some reports are forged; the regularity of the laws of nature argue against them; and the fact of the regular course of events undermines them.

Some of what Hume has here is just good common sense and rightly commends us to be wary of miracle stories. Hume's last two points refer to the same concern. If one were to weigh claims side by side, and one claim is exceedingly rare and the competing claim happens regularly, then without further evidence we ought to be persuaded by the weight of what happens habitually. So, say my employee is always punctual without fail. Then, when a customer claims that he was late, I ought to be suspicious of the claim.

But we have to be very careful about how we consider claims in light of Hume's credibility calculus. Say Mary has dated fifteen men over the last ten years. And she tells me that she just got engaged. Am I really to imagine that she shouldn't be believed because the odds against this most recent boyfriend asking for her hand is fifteen-to-one? One might say, well, the difference is that in this case it is not at all unusual for women to get engaged sometime. But the problem remains even in terms of the extraordinary. Say a friend says to me, "Something extraordinary happened to me." And I say, "That can't be believed. Since the vast number of our experiences are not extraordinary, there is overwhelming counter-evidence against your claim." Wouldn't my friend retort, "That's exactly what makes it extraordinary!" Do you see? Hume has stacked the deck. The very nature of a miracle is that it is irregular. So to say that because it is irregular it cannot be believed is to create a circular argument.

There is yet another problem with Hume's assumptions, and it is a liability shared by skeptics and indeed so many religious believers—that is, the assumption that God has intervened and broken the laws of nature. Physicist and Anglican priest John Polkinghorne writes, "Miracles are not to be interpreted as divine acts against the laws of nature (for these laws are themselves expressions of God's will) but as more profound revelations of the character of the divine relationship to creation."[205]

The most influential Roman Catholic theologian in the twentieth century was Karl Rahner. Rahner, following Aquinas, understood the created universe as a unity of matter and spirit, the lower and higher dimensions. Rahner argued that these dimensions are structured so that the higher dimension manifests itself in the lower without violating the lower. The integrity of both dimensions is maintained, but the lower is in itself not equipped to offer an explanation for the higher. So science is not violated when the higher realm engages it in a particular way. But science, which is only devised to explain the lower, would not know what to do about this. This is the position of many theologians today.[206] As Aquinas would say, miracles are *praeter naturam* (beyond physical nature) not *contra naturam* (violation of physical nature). The insight of the created world having both a spiritual quality as well as the physical is not new to some of the modern world's best philosophers and physicists.

Einstein discovered this long ago: "Everyone who is seriously involved in the pursuit of science becomes convinced that a spirit is manifest in the universe—a spirit that is vastly superior to that of man, and in the face of which we, with our modest powers, must feel humble."[207] Einstein was followed by Werner Heisenberg, who wrote, "The source of our knowledge is a numinous experience, an intuitive insight that is incommensurable with the functioning of the ordinary, dualistic mind."[208] He would later teach that our function in the universe is to bring about a relationship between the phenomenal and spiritual worlds—to look at them both simultaneously.[209]

Scientist and philosopher Alfred North Whitehead saw this, too: "The reason for the blindness of physical science is the fact that it only deals with half of the evidence provided by human experience. It divides the seamless coat—or to put it more positively, it examines the coat, which is superficial, and neglects the body, which is fundamental."[210]

Consider this case: In 1902, Dr. Alexis Carrel traveled to Lourdes to investigate reports of extraordinary healings, which he did not believe could be possible. During the journey he was asked to care for Marie Bailly, who was dying of advanced tuberculosis. He described her condition to a friend on the train: "This unfortunate girl is in the last stages of tubercular peritonitis. I know her history. Her whole family died of tuberculosis. She had tubercular sores, lesions of the lungs, and now for the last few months a peritonitis diagnosed both by a general practitioner and by the well-known Bordeaux surgeon, Bormilloux. Her condition is very grave....She might die at any moment right under my nose. If such a case as hers were cured, it would indeed be a miracle. I would never doubt again; I would become a monk."[211]

Bailly was carried to the grotto but not placed in the water, which they feared would kill her. Carrel kept a detailed record:

> *Condition very serious....Abdomen very sore and distended. Pulse irregular, low, almost imperceptible at 160; respiration jerky at 90; face contracted very pale and slightly cyanosed.*

Nose, ears, extremities cold. Dr. Geoffray of Rive-de-Gare arrives, he looked at the girl, feels, strikes, and ausculates the heart and lungs and pronounces her in the last agony. As there is nothing to be lost and the patient wishes to go to the grotto again, she is taken there on the stretcher.

At the grotto she was healed. Carrel and several other physicians examined her carefully at the Lourdes Medical Bureau where their signed attestations are on record. The physicians' report reads, "May 28, 7 PM. Our stupefaction was profound on seeing the girl who was so ill this morning sitting on her bed, chatting with nurses and answering our questions smilingly, also at seeing the enormous swelling of the abdomen had disappeared. The tumors which had encumbered it had melted away visibly, respiration and heart had resumed their normal play. This is a sudden, wonderful cure, a veritable resurrection." Geoffray added in his own hand: "This medical authentication which I am signing is the simple truth; so grave an affliction has never been cured in a few hours like the case on record here."[212] Ten years later, Carrel won the Nobel Prize in physiology and medicine for his advancements in surgery.

Here is a brief example of Joachime Dehant, a twenty-nine-year-old Belgian woman who made a pilgrimage to Lourdes in 1878. She had a massive gangrenous ulcer (twelve inches by six inches) on her right leg, an ulcer that penetrated to the bone, destroying muscles and tendons and causing her foot to invert. She had been attended by physicians for twelve years. On the trip, the stench from her wound so sickened her traveling companions on the train that several of them vomited. On her second bathing in the pool, she was healed; muscles, tendons, and skin were restored, leaving a well-formed scar. This cure was attested by physicians at Lourdes, her traveling companions, the citizens of Gesves, Belgium, where she lived all her life, by physicians who had treated her at Gesves, and by her family.[213]

I will address one more. In 1917 just outside of Fatima, Portugal, three schoolchildren had claimed that the Blessed Mother of Jesus appeared to them on July 13, August 19, and September 13, and that she promised on October 13 a miracle was going to occur at noon. There was something about the witness of these children that made them credible to the people of Fatima. Many other locals derided the whole seemingly absurd spectacle. The morning of October 13, 1917, tens of thousands of people went to the site. (One report was that the number was 30,000 to 40,000 and another report had the crowd at 100,000.) Late that morning there was a downfall of rain. At noon the clouds broke and the people witnessed the sun as an opaque spinning disc in the sky. It was multicolored and cast a rainbow of colors on the landscape and people. The sun then was reported to have careened toward the earth in a zigzag pattern. The sun performed such maneuvers for ten full minutes. Thousands of witnesses reported that their previously wet clothes were now completely dry and the soaked, muddy ground was also completely dry.

Given that the children did not themselves know what the miracle was going to be; given that many of the witnesses were skeptics, including representatives of news media who had been ridiculing the whole spectacle of the children's claims for three months; given that the number who confirmed the experience was the whole of the tens of thousands (with no dissenters!); given this, isn't there a compelling reason to believe that miracles are really quite possible?

Theologian Terence Nichols concludes, "There are thousands of stories like this. Of course everyone knows about auto-suggestion where a crippled person flings his crutches, only to collapse a half-hour later after the adrenalin wears off; and of course fraud. But thousands of other cases are authenticated with daunting evidence that it is unreasonable to dismiss them."[214] I might add, it is anti-intellectual and anti-scientific to dismiss them.

Show Me Your Soul

Earlier I explained a materialist's typical version of consciousness. Since materialists believe only physical things exist, consciousness cannot exist beyond the machinations of the physical brain. Carl Sagan and many others have described the brain as a computer or information processing center. This is the broad assumption in neuroscience. There is no spirit, no soul, no personal identity outside of the impersonal nerve cells. We hear from Francis Crick, himself so often quoted by atheists, "You, your joys and your sorrows, your memories and your ambitions, your sense of personal identity and free will, are in fact no more than the behavior of the vast assembly of nerve cells and their associated molecules."[215] Could this be true? Or if we do have souls or some kind of immaterial consciousness, how would you know?

As we have seen, materialists' versions of consciousness and free will turn out to be underwhelming and unaligned to our actual experience. But they rightly challenge religious believers: Give evidence for a soul. I'd like to suggest two pieces of evidence, one of which points to a consciousness that affects things outside of the physical brain. And the second is a soul that is independent in some clear manner from the physical body. It could also be that consciousness is the same as soul, and this would be satisfactory to the religious position.

Telepathic and Psychokinetic Phenomena

Is telepathy—that ability for consciousnesses to join one another outside of direct, physical experience of the other—real? Allow me a personal story. In 1995, I participated in a three-month silent retreat in a Buddhist retreat center in Barre, Massachusetts. Some were practicing loving-kindness meditation many hours a day. Here one places meditation subjects in one's mind's eye and offers them loving-kindness. Throughout a meditation period, one extends that loving-kindness progressively to the entire universe. One begins with a subject that one would have unadulterated love for. A fellow retreat member used her grandfather for this, since she adored her grandfather from her childhood on. For the first six weeks of the retreat, her meditation experience was very strong and incredibly gratifying. All of a sudden, on a Friday, she had great difficulty concentrating. She wondered what went wrong. Her meditation teacher told her not to be concerned and just stay the course. For two days she continued to have great difficulty engaging this meditation. Late Sunday, her meditation shut down completely. She felt strangely lost and sad. On Monday, her mother called her from California to tell her that her grandfather had suffered a stroke on Friday and subsequently died on Sunday. She flew back home, attended the funeral, mourned with her family, and then returned to the retreat to complete the final six or so weeks.

Are we really to believe that this was an utter coincidence? How was a level of her consciousness participating in her grandfather's? My hunch is that many know of other such stories like it. But the story only makes sense if our consciousness is not restricted to the physical brain. Actually, many such occurrences have been authenticated. Alan Turing, the father of artificial intelligence and one who imagined the brain in computational terms, wrote about them, "These disturbing phenomena seem to deny all our usual scientific ideas. How we should like to discredit them! Unfortunately the statistical evidence, at least for telepathy, is overwhelming."[216]

The existence of psychokinetic phenomena is also well verified scientifically. From 1974 through 1997 the results of about 2,250 ganzfeld (sensory deprivation) sessions were reported in at least forty publications by scientists worldwide. These studies focus on placing subjects in sensory deprivation experiments in which the subject must guess which of four mental images another subject in another deprivation room experienced at the same time. Researchers also typically used computer-generated images (autoganzfeld) to avoid contamination by human interventions ("the greasy finger effect"). Of course, the volunteers were often wrong. But if you had each of the volunteers perform, say, 100 speculations, then your data base is close to a quarter of a million times. That many times, you are statistically guaranteed that if it were only luck then the subjects would be right only 25 percent of the time. But they were right significantly more often. A meta-analysis of all Ganzfeld Telepathy Studies revealed the probability of a million billion to one against chance.[217]

We see the same fantastic results with psychokinesis, whereby the mind or consciousness has the power to affect something outside of it. For example, using a random number generator (RNG) that randomly flips an electronic "coin," the subject is told to influence the RNG by "wishing" for a one or zero. Of course the subjects were relatively close to fifty-fifty in results. But they were statistically clearly better than fifty-fifty. As Beauregard writes, "A small but stable effect has been shown over sixty years of tossing dice and RNGs that is reliable irrespective of the subject or the experimenter and remains when independent or skeptical investigators participate. A meta-analysis looking at 832 RNG studies conducted during the last decades showed odds against chance beyond a trillion to one."[218]

Our conclusions here can be modest. They are only that the mind is clearly not purely physical and clearly less tightly bound in space than a scientific materialist insists, and that there is something beyond merely neurons in the brain, something beyond the confines of the brain and the body.

Near-Death Experiences

In his 1975 classic *Life After Life: The Investigation of a Phenomenon—Survival of Bodily Death*, Dr. Raymond Moody collected 150 accounts of persons who nearly died or were clinically dead and were resuscitated, and who reported extraordinary experiences. Some of the common features of these near-death experiences (NDE) include: seeing themselves rise from their bodies; being able to describe things that could only be known from the vantage point above the heads of those present; feeling themselves pulled into a dark kind of tunnel and progressively drawing near to a brilliant light that radiated love; experiencing extraordinary peace; reviewing their lives, including the effects their actions had on others; encountering dead loved ones—even those they did not know were dead; being told to return to their bodies and earthly lives as their work was not yet done; and returning to their lives now more spiritually engaged, less materialistic, and more altruistic.

How are these to be explained by a materialist? Answers have included a lack of oxygen to the brain, endorphins, hallucinations, residual consciousness in the comatose patient, and so on. These explanations do not fit the evidence. Many patients who had NDEs were in the hospital where their blood oxygen was not cut off. Endorphins relax but do not create hallucinations. Hallucinations vary utterly, while NDEs do not. Comatose patients may hear things in a hospital on some level, but they don't see things, and no one gets to see things outside of one's visual range. It is also the case that some NDEs involve patients who have been hooked up to EEG machines that registered no brain activity whatsoever. From where do these perceptions and experiences come?[219]

The great Elisabeth Kübler-Ross, in her 1969 classic *On Death and Dying*, made it clear that she did not then believe in the afterlife, and that she imagined this projection a wish-fulfillment project. Through her subsequent years of research, she encountered some striking testimony that changed her mind. Kübler-Ross studied thousands of patients around the world who had NDEs. She found a legion of examples where accident victims could relate minute details of the event and subsequent rescue from perspectives impossible for their bodies to have been present to. She even found blind patients describing events visually. She encountered reports from patients who related meeting distant dead loved ones whom they had no idea were even dead until they met them during their NDE. Kübler-Ross writes, "Coincidence? By now there is no scientist or statistician who could convince me that this occurs, as some colleagues claim, as a result of 'oxygen deprivation' or for other 'rational and scientific' reasons."[220] There have been other scientific studies on NDEs by highly respected physicians, all with similar results.[221]

A fascinating NDE is recounted in the BBC-produced *The Day I Died*. Here we find Pam Reynolds, who was diagnosed as having a large aneurysm at the base of her brain. What Dr. Robert Spetzler, the director of the Barrow Neurological Institute in Phoenix, did was to chill her body between 50–60 degrees, stopping all heart and brain activity, and then to drain her blood from the brain. Then the aneurysm was repaired, the blood pumped back into the patient, and the heart restarted. Reynolds' eyelids were taped shut and speakers were placed in her ears, which emitted repeated loud clicks to test the responsiveness of the auditory nerve in her brain stem. So even if she had been conscious, she would not have been able to hear or see anything. But she was more than unconscious. Her heart and brain functions were completely stopped, and instruments properly showed no brain activity. Reynolds reported a full NDE, including the dynamics of the surgery that involved conversations among the surgeons, complications and how they solved them, and even the tools used.

How do the materialists account for no brain activity, no heartbeat, no blood in her system, no chemicals floating anywhere?[222]

One of the most interesting reports of an NDE has to do with A. J. Ayer, perhaps the most famous intellectual atheist in Britain during the twentieth century. In 1988, Ayer had two near death experiences. He wrote about them in the *London Daily Telegraph*, including his experience of being confronted by a light that he said "was responsible for the government of the universe." Three months later he was alarmed by the worldwide publicity, which included a front-page headline in the *National Enquirer* titled "Afterlife Shocker." Ayer retreated from his original witness in public, but in private he had confided in his physician, Dr. Jeremy George, that he had encountered the "Divine Being." Dr. George kept this private during Ayer's life as he considered it a confidential confession. Interestingly, Ayer's family and friends found him a far kinder, gentler person after this spiritual experience. "He became so much nicer after he died," his wife declared. Ayer also began spending a great deal of time with Fr. Frederick Copleston, his former debating opponent. "In the end," his wife, Dee, said, "he [Copleston] was Freddie's [Ayer] closest friend. It was quite extraordinary."[223]

I do not claim to know exactly what a soul is, or consciousness, or the relationship between the soul and body, or that between consciousness and the brain. But the evidence that we have touched on here tells me that the religious account aligns exactly with these scientific, fact-driven, evidence-based studies, and that they all point decidedly to some kind of soul or consciousness that is not material. One can embrace scientific materialism if one wants. But this would be at the cost of running away from an enormous amount of scientific evidence.

Chapter Eight

Proving God

Addressing the Hidden God

As a child, the Hasidic Master of Lublin used to go out into the woods. "What are you looking for out there?" his father asked. "I am looking for God." "Isn't God everywhere, and isn't God everywhere the same?" "He is," replied the child, "but I am not."

HASIDIC TALE

The great atheist philosopher Bertrand Russell was once asked what he would say if he died and did discover God, who now wanted to know why Russell hadn't believed in him. Russell's response was, "Not enough evidence, God, not enough evidence."[224] As we have seen, meaning, truth, and goodness point to a transcendent ground, that is, God. Indeed, our very ability to assess such things and our confidence that we can have a modicum of success in doing so points to God as well. We also have to remember that God is nonphysical (*incorporeal*) and not a member of the universe (*transcendent*). So, we would not be experiencing God through physical ways of perceiving, and our evidence has to be mindful of this.

How does a religious response address this mystery? Pascal writes, "What can be seen on earth indicates neither total absence, nor manifest presence of divinity, but the presence of a hidden God. Everything bears his stamp."[225] This sums up the religious perspective.

I see a number of good reasons why God's presence is both available and hidden. One is that the problem is not with God, but with us. Because of our spiritual immaturity, we do not see the divine presence before us as clearly as we ought to. Recall that William James points out that seeing and understanding things has a history in our experience, and that knowledge is both subjective and objective at the same time. Further, some people are in a better position to see something because they have cultivated that form of knowledge, that way of perception. A literary professor sees the depth of Shakespeare better than one who is uncultured.

Pascal's Real Wager[226]

Getting near to God is what Blaise Pascal was getting at with his famous *Wager*, something often completely misunderstood. Pascal challenges us to consider life as a wager. Many skeptics (and some religious interpreters) imagine the wager as this: If you believe in God and you're right, you will go to heaven, but if you're wrong, you lose little. If you do not believe in God and you're right, there is no real reward, but if you're wrong, you go to hell. So, belief in God is the rational bet. This isn't really Pascal's wager at all. Pascal begins his wager argument with this striking passage:

> *Either God is or he is not. But to which view shall we be inclined? Reason cannot decide this question. Infinite chaos separates us. At the far end of this infinite distance a coin is being spun and which will come down heads or tails. How would you wager? Reason cannot make you choose either, reason cannot prove either wrong.*[227]

If you read through the whole of his *Pensées* ("Thoughts"), many passages make it clear that Pascal thought there was a great deal of authentic, compelling evidence for God and religious faith. But the evidence is not going to be gained as if from a cold, hard rational look at the facts. Like James, Pascal also believed that human beings are rarely unbiased in their interpretations of reality. Further, our lives are either inclined toward knowledge of God or away from knowledge of God. So by the way we are conducting our lives we are already implicitly betting about God. To the degree that your life is in intense pursuit of the true and the good, that you have placed your life in the service of something beyond yourself, you are implicitly betting on God. To the degree that your life is in intense pursuit of your ego's interests, a failure to seek or place your life under the demands of the good and the true, you are implicitly betting against God. To this latter life Pascal will ask, "To what advantage?"[228]

Pascal fully recognized that you cannot will to believe something that hasn't convinced your intellect. But he also wants us to face the fact that if we are living a life decidedly away from God, we are progressively losing our ability to come to know God in the future. In many places in his *Pensées*, he charges us to look closely and honestly at the state of our souls.

> **Unbeliever**: *Yes, but my hands are tied and my lips are sealed; I am forced to wager and I am not free; I am being held fast and I am so made that I cannot believe. What do you want me to do then?*
>
> **Pascal**: *That is true, but at least get it into your head that, if you were unable to believe, it is because of your passions.... Concentrate then not on convincing yourself by multiplying proofs of God's existence but by diminishing your passions. You want to find faith and you do not know the road. You want to be cured of unbelief and you ask for a remedy: Learn from those who were once bound like you and who now wager all they have. These are people who know the road you wish*

to follow, who have been cured of the affliction of which you wish to be cured: Follow the way by which they began.[229]

The two sides of his wager that he points us to represent a life of sin and a life of virtue, or better, a life of affliction and a life of health. Look toward those who are healthy, he says, those who have been cured. These are the people who are "all in" regarding their wager. That is, they really have given all they had and are to faith in God. "These are the people who know the road" to holiness and joy. Follow that way. So, belief is not something you can will. But walking the road *toward* God is the kind of behavior that will offer the best possibility to know God. As philosopher Thomas Morris says, "The discernment of spiritual truth may also require certain capacities that in most of us desperately need cultivating. Pascalian wagering is best viewed as a determined attempt to cultivate those capacities on the part of people who, because of the great values involved, are gambling their lives, hoping for success."[230]

The issue isn't about betting, really, but about a life that is either conditioning itself to know God or miss God completely. The evidence then accumulates as one walks the road of faith. And the main evidence is what a faithful lifestyle brings. Pascal writes, "A Christian's hope of possessing an infinite good is mingled with actual enjoyment....Christians hope for holiness, and to be freed from unrighteousness, and some part of this is theirs already."[231] What harm will come to you if you make this choice? Pascal asks. You will renounce "tainted pleasures." Instead, "You will be faithful, honest, humble, grateful, a doer of good works, a good friend, sincere and true."[232] John Cottingham says of Pascal, "The carrot is not pie in the sky as the goal of spiritual transformation."[233]

Pascal is *not* posing God as the safe eternal bet, and certainly *not* creating an argument for God's existence, and again *not* providing an argument designed to produce immediate faith.

Rather, he uses wagering language to clarify that we are already implicitly betting with our lives in the way we live them and to show the way to discover God. The evidence comes while walking the path.

Sensus Divinitatis

Philosopher Alvin Plantinga argues with enormous intellectual depth for a knowing faculty he calls the *sensus divinitatis*, the ability to intuit God in one's heart and mind.[234] There is a way of knowing built into the human psyche that can recognize and experience transcendental truths. This cannot be utterly aligned to a materialistic understanding of the brain, which is only geared to the natural world, but it surely is not divorced from the brain and its workings. Plantinga demonstrates that when this faculty is working well, when it is cultivated and one is receptive to its workings, then the divine presence is not obscure at all.

For Thomas Aquinas, knowing God is a progressive adventure and requires engagement. Aquinas uses an example of seeing something far off. Initially, it is an indistinguishable blur, but as one nears, one sees it is an animal, then a man, then one's friend. We see in his example that the basic focus has not changed, but one's progressive understanding has. To the degree that we embrace what is transcendent, we are implicitly encountering God. Initially, it is blurry, but as we progress toward the good and true our experience of the divine becomes increasingly direct.[235] In this case one's *sensus divinitatis* is both natural (seeking authentic happiness by what is good and true) and supernatural (grounded in and directed toward God).

We might also consider the spiritual journey as one from greater obscurity to greater clarity regarding God's omnipresence. Religions widely describe this dynamic. God is initially experienced quite indirectly, even vaguely. As we grow in interiority, we come progressively to experience God more directly and immediately. There is a wonderfully insightful line in John's Gospel where Jesus tells Nicodemus, "No one can see the kingdom of God without being born from above" (John 3:3). That is, if you want to see the divine reality, you need first to experience spiritual transformation. It doesn't mean compelling evidence does not exist; it means that one must not be naïve about how to encounter it and the cost of the encounter.

Aquinas' Proofs for God

> *The odds against a universe like ours emerging out of something like the Big Bang are enormous. I think there are clearly religious implications.*[236] *...It would be very difficult to explain why the universe would have begun in just this way except as the act of God who intended to create beings like us.*
>
> STEPHEN HAWKING [237]

It has become fashionable to rehash medieval proofs for the existence of God, to deconstruct them, and then to declare victory over theists. Typically religious opponents misunderstand them. I think these arguments are incredibly useful. My shorthand of Thomas Aquinas' proofs for the existence of God follows:

First argument is first mover: Some things are in motion and anything moved is moved by something else. Since there cannot be movers in an infinite series, there must be a first mover who itself is not moved by another. This is God. *Second argument is first cause*: Some things are caused and anything caused is caused by something else. Since there cannot be causes in an infinite series, there must be a first cause itself not caused by another. This is God. *Third argument is necessary being*: Every contingent being at some time did not exist. If every being were contingent, then nothing would exist at one time. Thus, there would be nothing now. Since this is false, there must be a necessary noncontingent being. This is God.

These three reference God as a necessary creator.

Fourth argument is greatest being: Things compare by degrees, such as more or less good or noble. The greatest in truth are the greatest in being and the reference from which that being exists and is understood. Therefore there must be something that causes all beings as well as their perfections. This is God.

Aquinas here is principally concerned with perfections, such as goodness. For us to appeal to something as a moral good is to necessarily draw on a nonperceptual, nonphysical category. To believe in objective goodness requires there to be both a ground from which to experience the goodness so as to know it is good, and a horizon on which to conceptually recognize the degree it participates in goodness itself. I have dealt with this argument throughout this book and will not address it here.

Fifth argument is intelligent designer: Unintelligent things act for an end that they cannot choose. They therefore must be directed by an intelligence not their own. Thus, the world must have an intelligent being directing their end. This is God.

Aquinas is not comparing God to a watchmaker where complexity could not have existed without God. (Evolution has a legitimate answer for this). Rather, he argues toward ends that created things do not have the capacity for self-generating.

Rethinking Aquinas' First Three Arguments

Aquinas' first three arguments are predicated on understanding the difference between conditioned and unconditioned reality, and their intrinsic relationship.[238] A "conditioned reality" is anything from an individual to a particle that depends on something for its existence to come about. A mouse, for example, is conditioned on cells and structures of cells for its existence. Those cells are conditioned on molecules and structures of molecules, which themselves are conditioned on atoms and structures of atoms. These then are conditioned on quarks and structures of quarks.

This is the case with everything in the physical world. "Unconditioned reality" would obviously be that which depends on no other reality for its existence, that is, God. Let's say atheists are right and that there is no unconditioned reality (God), but only conditioned realities (things). Then this conditioned thing would have to depend on an infinite number of conditions, since those conditions would need preceding conditions *ad infinitum*. There has to be at least one unconditioned reality that grounds any other conditioned reality for that other reality to achieve existence. So until all these infinite conditions are met, and they can't be met as they are infinite, a mouse would never come about. Nothing would! Aquinas is just getting started.

Aquinas was also convinced that an infinite regress of time was unreasonable. He was relying on a theory of physics we do not hold. And yet his intuitions are confirmed even more strongly by modern physics. Thinking about time before the Big Bang doesn't work well, as time and space are intimately related. We typically imagine that, as the universe expands, galaxies are moving in space. Now the consensus, begun by Einstein and broadly confirmed in physics, is that galaxies are getting farther apart because the space in between them is getting stretched out. Extrapolating the space back is how cosmologists have determined that the universe is 13.7 billion years old. Other discoveries have supported and fine-tuned all this. Some kind of everlasting time before the Big Bang turns out to be a bad question, because there was no time or space, no measurement outside of the universe. As it turns out, Einstein strengthens Aquinas' philosophical intuitions considerably.

Are there other ways to get out of the conclusion that there was a creator of the universe? Some have been tried. One is a bouncing universe theory positing that eternally the universe expands then collapses, then another Big Bang expansion to collapse, and so on, eternally. A version of this is that part of the universe is doing this—the part that we are in.[239] Neither of these works, and for several reasons. One reason has to do with the relationship between the light of Cosmic Background Radiation (CBR) left over from the Big Bang and light from other sources, especially stars. In our universe we have 99 percent CBR and 1 percent starlight. If a bounce happened, then the starlight would lose a percentage of its emitting power and the CBR would gain light. If there were a thousand bounces, there would have to be at least 1,000 times more light in CBR than starlight. So there could only have been at most 100 bounces to arrive at the current status, and if there had been bounces from eternity, there would simply be no starlight at all. Entropy, the law that all matter moves from concentration to dissipation, also ensures that stellar dissipation increases with every bounce cycle. So an infinite cycle guarantees no stars for this additional reason.

Some physicists have wondered whether one could find a solution regarding Einstein's equations of gravity where the Big Bang Singularity (the starting point) could be traced back infinitely into the past. Stephen Hawking and Roger Penrose proved otherwise. Others postulated that near such singularities the classical description of gravity was no longer valid, thus opening possibilities that the Big Bang was itself the beginning of the universe (no first cause outside of it) or that the Big Bang is a portal to an era that preceded it. Following on the work of Hawking-Penrose, Borde-Vilenkin-Guth collectively showed that all known mathematical configurations that would allow for some portal, etc., would require a beginning. They discovered that every model where a universe could happen had to have a temporal boundary. As Alex Vilenkin wrote, "With the proof now in place, cosmologists can no longer hide behind the possibility of a past-eternal universe. There is no escape, they have to face the problem of a cosmic beginning."[240]

Argument by Design

The argument from design also remains compelling from the results of modern science. It was the noted atheist philosopher Antony Flew who in 2004 became a theist on the weight of the DNA complexity required of the arrangements that are needed to produce life. Flew thought that supernatural intelligence must have been involved. With regard to human life, Flew asked, "How can a universe of mindless matter produce beings with intrinsic ends, self-replication capacities and coded chemistry? We are not dealing with biology, but an entirely different category of problem."[241] It was life itself that convinced Flew: "My one and only piece of relevant evidence [for God] is the apparent impossibility of providing a naturalistic theory of the origin from DNA of the first reproducing species....The only reason which I have for beginning to think of believing in a First-Cause god is the impossibility of proving a naturalistic account of the origin of the first reproducing organisms."[242]

Another biological or evolutionary tack is to consider human life or consciousness. I've done this throughout the book. While I accept evolution, I have challenged scientism, materialism, and the theory that evolution is the only dynamic in human development. These atheistic dogmas do not at all cohere with human consciousness, with moral intuitions, or with confidence in securing the truth. But it certainly does seem that our consciousness is wired for transcendence. We are intrinsically wired for truth and goodness that is beyond ourselves and beyond what materialism or evolution could ever provide. This is what Aquinas was getting at.

By far the most interesting and compelling arguments by design are focused on physics and cosmology. Accepting all the latest, best work in physics, theistic philosophers believe that the evidence strongly points to God intelligently providing the possibility for life against all odds. This is called the "anthropic principle." The small number of total possible mass energy interactions in the universe for all time reveals the extreme improbability of high degrees of complexity coming out of the universe by pure chance. This has led some physicists to see the prospect of an intelligent design creator as the most plausible explanation. The list of such physicists is impressive and includes Roger Penrose, Arno Penzias, Owen Gingerich, John Polkinghorne, Fred Hoyle, and Paul Davies.[243] As Davies writes, "It is hard to resist the impression that the present structure of the universe, apparently so sensitive to minor alterations in the numbers, has been rather carefully thought out....The seemingly miraculous concurrence of numerical values that nature has assigned to her fundamental constants must remain the most compelling evidence for an element of cosmic design."[244]

These are the noncontroversial constants of the universe as it relates to the Big Bang:[245]

1. Minimum interval of space: 1.62 times 10 to the minus 33rd power cm
3. Minimum unit of time: 5.39 times 10 to the minus 44th second
4. Planck's constant for frequency of light: 66 times 10 to the minus 34th joule seconds
5. Speed of light: 300,000 km/second
6. Gravitational attraction constant: 6.67 times 10 to the minus 11th power
7. Weak force coupling constant 1.43 times 10 to the minus 62nd power
8. Strong nuclear force coupling constant: 15
9. Rest mass of a proton: 1.67 times 10 to the minus 27th kg
10. Rest mass of an electron: 9.11 times 10 to the minus 31st kg
11. Electron or proton unit charge: 1.6 times 10 to the minus 19th coulombs

12. Minimum mass of the universe: 2.18 times 10 to the minus 8th kg
13. Amount of energy and total amount of rest related to it: rest mass thought to be 10 53rd kg
14. Boltzmann's constant: 1.38 times 10 to the minus 23rd J/K
15. Hubble constant: 2 times 10 to the minus 18th (SI units)
16. Cosmological constant: less than 10 to the minus 53rd (SI units)
16. Cosmit photo/proton ratio: 10 to the 9th (SI units)
17. Permittivity of free space: 8.85 times 10 to the minus 12th (SI units)
18. Electromagnetic fine-structure constant: 7.30 times 10 to the minus 3rd (SI units)
19. Weak fine-structure constant: 3.05 times 10 to the minus 12th (Si units)
20. Gravitational fine-structure constant: 5.90 times ten to the minus 39th (SI Units)

Francis Collins, in addressing fifteen of these constants, writes:

> *When you look from the perspective of a scientist at the universe, it looks like it knew we were coming. There are fifteen constants—the gravitational constant, various constants about strong and weak nuclear force, etc.,—that have precise values. If any one of these constants was off by one part in a million, or in some cases by one part in a million million, the universe could not have actually come to the point where we see it. Matter would not have been able to coalesce, there would have been no galaxy, stars, planets, or people.*[246]

According to Penrose, the odds of the universe surviving as a universe without its recollapsing or failing to allow matter to form, etc., are 1 in 10 to the 10th to the 123rd. This is an unimaginably long number. The odds are, for all intents and purposes, utterly impossible.

Recall our version of Ockham's razor: that preference for the explanation that is simplest and most elegant, that takes into account the most data, and is most coherent about the most critical data. Given this, how do atheistic accounts fare? Not well. Removing the explanations that modern physics has proven impossible, Richard Dawkins is satisfied with the following: We're lucky.[247] Plantinga imagines this argument at a poker game in the old West. You deal yourself 1,000 hands in a row of four aces and take everyone's money in the county. They challenge you for cheating, and your response is, "We're just lucky enough to be in the particular universe where I deal myself thousands of four-ace poker hands in a row, all by plain ol' luck." And the next words heard are, "String him up."[248] No one accepts this argument in any other issue, particularly regarding scientific concerns. Philosopher of science Bruce Gordon concludes:

> *When the logical and metaphysical necessity of an efficient cause, the demonstrable absence of a material one, and the proof that there was an absolute beginning to any universe or multiverses are all conjoined with the fact that our universe exists and its conditions are fine-tuned immeasurably beyond the capacity of any mindless process, the scientific evidence points inexorably toward transcendent intelligent agency as the most plausible, if not the only reasonable explanation.*[249]

Conclusion

Two Versions of Reality

In the beginning of this book I told you I would be offering you two versions of reality: that of New Atheists, along with their scientific materialist friends, and that of religious believers. Evidence is one of their key concerns, and they tell us that religions make extraordinary claims but produce no evidence. I want to make clear that thoughtful religious believers do think evidence is a good and necessary thing and part of the reason why some religious perspectives ought to be rejected and others affirmed. So the religious version is big on evidence, too, but it wants to look at all the evidence and not just reduce everything to scientific materiality. Indeed, some issues are particularly vexing for science, such as consciousness and freedom, as we have seen. I also asked you to consider how well the material is interpreted. As you've been reading this book, I've asked you to consider which version is more plausible and coherent.

The version of scientific materialism is, as we have seen, devoid of much evidence. Evolutionary psychology lacks evidence as a virtual methodological principle. It takes the assumptions of evolution, ignores any other causal issues to consider, and then imagines a plausible story to explain things as they are now. Typically the story includes making claims about prehistoric humans with no data set whatsoever and conjectures about memes, themselves lacking scientific methodology or even evidence itself.

If the New Atheists' story of scientific materialism is to be persuasive, then a religious version of the universe must be the enemy, the direct competitor to be killed off. So New Atheism has told us things that simply are not true. We have been given an impossibly skewed revision of real history. We have experienced correlations between religion and immorality and violence that do not hold. And we have been told really odd things about religion that are simply made up out of whole cloth. Finally, we have encountered odd arguments, poor arguments, and straw man arguments. In short, we've been offered willful misinterpretations of the facts, manipulated data, and purely contrived claims. New Atheists regularly challenge that religions create their beliefs irrationally. I hope you see that it is they who have been doing this all along.

The religious version is one where evidence includes that of human experience. For us, wonder corresponds to a transcendental quality of the mind itself—that we are structured for transcendence. The religious version says that our experience and engagement in the world is not meaningless but rather filled with value because it both has a transcendental ground and an end, a place where it is going. In a meaningless universe where evolution is the only thing driving existence, we should oppress the weak. But we know that we should not. We know that something has placed a moral demand on us, that the human race is one family, each member sharing the same intrinsic value. Rather than a blind, irrational, and random world that is the world of materialism, the religious world is one of intelligibility. It is personal and purposeful. All our best intuitions point to God.

When they demand that we show them what is outside of chemistry and neurons, we ask, does a collection of impersonal atoms have free will? Do they love? When materialists say there is no real free will, no objective morality, no real self, we say, none of you actually lives as if that's really true, none of you. When we look at physics and cosmology and the impossible odds against existence, we see daunting evidence for an intelligent creator. New Atheists see the impossible odds of dumb luck.

Both authentically religious people and skeptics alike find religious dogmatism and intolerance a serious problem. By nature, they are anti-intellectual and represent a threat to a personal mature religious faith as well as human unity. It is a fear-based religious style that advocates a "we vs. them" mentality, even if that only involves religious ideology. It should also be clear that both New Atheists and I believe in science, and that scientific inquiry should always retain its independent methods and conclusions. (The Catholic Church insists on it!) Finally, we all agree that religions can be used in part to contrast humans in a negative way. Like ethnic or national identities, religious identities can be used to justify aggression, whether that be derision, discrimination, or something more heinous. Let's call the first concern an enemy of reason and mutual understanding, the second an enemy of knowledge, and the third an enemy of public welfare.

Given this, I am particularly disturbed by New Atheism, because it is a movement that aids and abets all three enemies. As we have seen, the message of New Atheists is that you have to choose: science or religion. This feeds religiously anti-science attitudes. Worse than this, I believe that this movement facilitates intolerance and prejudice. We saw this regarding Islamophobia. Such hate speech advances enemies of reason and authentic religion.

Recall the invisible gorilla from the introduction. There is nothing more obvious than the gorilla on the basketball court. But a good half of the viewers were so intent on watching the passing game that they simply didn't register what they were not looking for, not psychologically available for.

For many religious believers, the truth about God is not hard to recognize. But if you're not looking for God or not open to God or even decidedly against experiencing God, then a psyche that would otherwise become conscious of God becomes one that is sure there is no God. Knowledge of the divine requires paying attention, a certain spacious mind and heart, an openness to listen to the myriad forms of evidence. God no longer becomes a mere hypothesis or gratuitous claim, but the Truth before us. God is right here, indeed the foundation and horizon of all that is good and true about us. But without attention to these many obvious signs, we end up seeing everything but God.

A final parable: There is a Muslim story about the sage Nasrudden. Always riding on a mule, Nasrudden kept going back and forth between one state and another. The constancy of his crossings convinced the border guards that he was involved in some trade without paying taxes. Every time he crossed, they fastidiously searched his packages, clothing, and even the mule's mouth to see what was being smuggled. They never found anything and were always obliged to let him pass. Many years later, one of the former border guards, now long retired, asked Nasrudden to come clean as to what he was trading. He smiled and simply said, "Mules."

Endnotes

1 John Hick, *The Fifth Dimension* (Oxford: Oneworld, 1999), 14.

2 As cited in Alvin Plantinga, "Dennett's Dangerous Idea: Evolution and the Meanings of Life," *Books and Culture* 2 (May/June 1996): 16–18.

3 Stephen Prothero, *Religious Literacy: What Every American Needs to Know—and Doesn't* (New York: HarperOne, 2007), 27ff., 55ff.

4 Robert Wright, *The Evolution of God* (New York: Little, Brown and Company, 2009), 444–45.

5 S.C. Hitchcock, *Disbelief 101: A Young Person's Guide to Atheism* (Tuscan: See Sharp Press, 2009).

6 Christopher Hitchens, *God Is Not Great: How Religion Poisons Everything* (New York: Twelve, 2007), 13.

7 Sam Harris, *Letter to a Christian Nation* (New York: Alfred A. Knopf, 2006), ix. See also Harris as cited by John Haught ("If anyone has written a book more critical of religious faith than I have, I'm not aware of it."), "Amateur Atheists: Why the New Atheism Isn't Serious," in *Christian Century* (February 26, 2008): 26.

8 It should be noted that Hitchens does not think this, and he himself finds Harris and Dawkins reductive here. On the other hand, he is an avowed materialist and has not provided any reason why Harris and Dawkins would be off here, given materialism.

9 Harris writes, for example, "[O]ur religious differences—and hence our religious belief—are antithetical to our survival.... Words like God and Allah must go the way of Apollo and Baal or they will unmake our world....The very idea of religious toleration is one of the principal forces driving us toward the abyss....Religions are not about discourse and [they] avoid sustained reason. The very tenets have immunized us against the power of conversation." Sam Harris, *The End of Faith: Religion, Terror, and the Future of Reason* (New York and London: W.W. Norton & Company, 2005), 14–15, 45. Such claims are rife through Hitchens and Dawkins as well.

10 This is detailed by the inventors of the *Invisible Gorilla Test* in their recent book. See Christopher Chabris and Daniel Simons, *The Invisible Gorilla: And Other Ways Our Intuitions Deceive Us* (New York: Crown, 2010). The point of the book is to challenge typical assumptions and often our own intuitions. *That* is not what I'm arguing in this book. My only point in using this book is to reference an image about not seeing what is before you when you aren't prepared or interested in seeing it. When prepared, it becomes quite obvious. This, to me, has an excellent analogy to God's presence.

11 Bertrand Russell, "An Outline of Intellectual Rubbish," in *The Portable Atheist: Essential Readings for the Nonbeliever*, ed. Christopher Hitchens (Philadelphia: De Capo Press, 2007), 181–206.

12 Harris, *The End of Faith*, 173.

13 Hitchens, *God Is Not Great*, 13.

14 *Ibid.*, 10.

15 Dawkins, *The God Delusion*, 51.

16 Terry Eagleton, *Reason, Faith, and Revolution: Reflections About the God Debate* (New Haven: Yale University Press, 2009), ix.

17 Hitchens, *God Is Not Great*, 13.

18 Harris, *The End of Faith*, 160.

19 Dawkins, *The God Delusion*, 63.

20 Harris, *The End of Faith*, 154; Dawkins, *The God Delusion*, 63.

21 Dennett, *Breaking the Spell*, 280.

22 Hitchens, *God Is Not Great*, 5.

23 Harris, *Letter to a Christian Nation*, 25.

24 2011: Ellen Johnson Sirleaf—Christian; Leymah Gbowee—Christian; Tawakkol Karman—Muslim; 2010: Liu Xiaobo—An apparent theist; 2009: Barack Obama—Christian; 2008: Martti Ahtisaari—Christian; 2007: Albert Gore—Christian; 2006: Muhammad Yunus—Muslim; 2005: Mohamed El-Baradei—Muslim; 2004: Wangari Maathai—Christian; 2003: Shirin Ebadi— Muslim; 2002: Jimmy Carter—Christian; 2001: Kofi Annan—Christian; 2000: Kim Dae-Jung—Christian; 1999: Doctors Without Borders; 1998: John Hume—Christian, and David Trimble—Christian; 1997: Jody Williams—unknown; 1996: Carlos Felipe Ximenes Belo—Christian, and Jose Ramos-Horta—Christian; 1995: Joseph Rotblat—Agnostic; 1994: Yasser Arafat—Muslim; Shimon Peres—Jewish; Yitzhak Rabin—Jewish; 1993: Nelson Mandela—Christian, and Fredrik Willem de Klerk—Christian; 1992: Rigoberta Menchu Tum—Christian; 1991: Augn San Suu Kyi—Buddhist; 1990: Mikhail Sergeyevich Gorbachev—None; 1989: Tenzin Gyatso (14th Dalai Lama)—Buddhist; 1988: UN Peace-Keeping Forces; 1987: Oscar Arias Sanchez—Christian; 1886: Elie Wiesel—Jewish; 1985: International Physicians for the Prevention of Nuclear War; 1984: Desmond Mpilo Tutu—Christian; 1983: Lech Walesa—Christian; 1982: Alva Myrdal—nonreligious; Alfonso Garcia Robles—Christian; 1981: Office of the United Nations High Commissioner for Refugees; 1980: Adolfo Perez Esquivel—Christian.

25 Arthur C. Brooks, "Religious Faith and Charitable Giving," *Policy Review* 121 (October/November, 2003), as cited in Beauregard and O'Leary, *The Spiritual Brain*, 247.

26 George H. Gallup, Jr., "Dogma Bites Man: On the New and Biased Research Linking Faith and Social Ills," *Touchstone* (December 2005): 62–63.

27 Dawkins, *The God Delusion*, 288–93.

28 Harris, *Letter to a Christian Nation*, 2, and approvingly quoted at length in Dawkins, *The God Delusion*, 342.

29 Hitchens, *God Is Not Great*, 13.

30 *Ibid.*, 200.

31 *Ibid.*, 223ff. According to UNICEF, 90 percent of all women are circumcised in Egypt, Mali, Guinea, and Sudan, while almost no women are circumcised in Iraq, Iran, and Saudi Arabia. In December 2006, a conference of high-ranking Muslim theologians, hosted by the Egyptian Grand Mufti Ali Gomaa, agreed that the practice of female genital mutilation is irreconcilable with Islam. What is important here is that they did not simply say it was non-Islamic—they said that it was opposed to authentic Islam. See John L. Esposito and Dalia Mogahed, *Who Speaks for Islam: What a Billion Muslims Really Think* (New York: Gallup Press, 2007), 117.

32 Hitchens, *God Is Not Great*, 283.

33 Harris, *The End of Faith*, 161–64.

34 Dawkins, *The God Delusion*, 112.

35 Hitchens, *God Is Not Great*, 56.

36 *Ibid.*, 133. What Hitchens says he is doing is helping us understand the process of *ijtihad*, categories of interpretation of Muhammad's sayings. But that process refers to a system of Islamic interpretations by which one extrapolates principles from the Quran and sayings or examples of the prophet, to apply them to a new cultural situation. This would be part

of making the faith relevant in a new time and place. So he's not even close. And the idea that a devout Muslim imagines authenticated sayings from the prophet as intentional falsehoods is beyond the pale.

37 See Dawkins, *The God Delusion*, 307; Hitchens, *God Is Not Great*, 180.

38 Hitchens, *God Is Not Great*, 176.

39 For details of the whole movement, I commend David Chappell's *A Stone of Hope: Prophetic Religion and the Death of Jim Crow* (Chapel Hill: University of North Carolina Press, 2003).

40 Harris, *The End of Faith*, 58, 73, 85; Dawkins, *The God Delusion*, 232; Hitchens, *God Is Not Great*, 71, 150.

41 Dawkins, *The God Delusion*, 232, 323.

42 Harris, *The End of Faith*, 66; *ibid.*, 65: "Faith is what credulity becomes when it finally achieves escape velocity from the constraints of terrestrial discourse—constraints like reasonableness, internal coherence, civility, and candor."

43 *Ibid.*, 105.

44 Pope John Paul II, *Fides et Ratio* (London: Catholic Truth Society, 1998), §16.

45 Dawkins, *The God Delusion*, 324, 335.

46 Hitchens, *God Is Not Great*, 111–12.

47 *Ibid.*, 120.

48 Harris, *The End of Faith*, 35, 45; *Letter to a Christian Nation*, 60–61.

49 Dennett, as interviewed in John Brockman, *The Third Culture* (New York: Touchstone Books, 1996), 187.

50 Hitchens, *God Is Not Great*, 11, 15.

51 Thomas Nagel, *The Last Word* (Oxford: Oxford University Press, 1997).

52 Some of this gloss material can be found in a number of texts. I'm relying on personal knowledge of the field as well as such texts as James Thrower, *Western Atheism: A Short History* (Amherst: Prometheus Books, 2000); Julian Baggini, *Atheism: A Very Short Introduction* (Oxford: Oxford University Press, 2003); and Michael Martin, ed., *The Cambridge Companion to Atheism* (Cambridge: Cambridge University Press, 2007).

53 Hitchens, *God Is Not Great*, 259.

54 Newton and Descartes did think that God, angels, and human will were not subject to those deterministic laws and could intervene or act on the world outside of mechanical laws. They differed from each other as to whether causes (agents) could affect other objects (patients) at a distance. Newton argued yes, while Descartes argued no.

55 Michael Buckley, *Denying and Disclosing God: The Ambitious Progress of Modern Atheism* (New Haven: Yale University Press, 2004), 35.

56 Baggini, *Atheism*, 79.

57 I am hardly the first to recognize this. See, for example, Alister McGrath, *The Twilight of Atheism: The Rise and Fall of Disbelief in the Modern World* (New York: Galilee, 2006), 180.

58 Dawkins, *The God Delusion*, 202, 209, 218.

59 These two quotes were taken from Albert Einstein, *The Expanded Quotable Einstein* (Princeton: Princeton University Press, 2000), 214, and "Science, Philosophy and Religion: A Symposium" (Conference on Science, Philosophy, and Religion in Their Relation to the Democratic Way of Life, Inc., New York, 1941), http://www.sacred-texts.com/aor/einstein/einsci.htm.

60 Dawkins, *The God Delusion*, 151.

61 Bertrand Russell, "An Outline of Intellectual Rubbish," in Christopher Hitchens, ed., *The Portable Atheist: Essential Readings for the Nonbeliever* (Philadelphia: Da Capo Press, 2007).

62 As cited in Dawkins, *The God Delusion*, 92. This was originally published in the August 2006 edition of *Playboy*.

63 Origen, for instance, thought that the literary genre of the Gospels was fundamentally historical. He also, along with so many others, saw that the infancy narratives in Matthew and Luke did not line up. His conclusion was that Luke's was historical while Matthew's was allegorical.

64 Karen Armstrong, *A Case for God* (New York and Toronto: Alfred A. Knopf, 2009), 186.

65 As cited in Buckley, *Denying and Disclosing God*, 8.

66 *Ibid.*, 12–13.

67 *Ibid.*, 20–22.

68 Ian Barbour, *Religion and Science* (San Francisco: Harper, 1997), 77–105.

69 Stephen Jay Gould, *Rock of Ages: Science and Religion in the Fullness of Life* (New York: Ballantine, 1999), 6.

70 Hitchens, *God Is Not Great*, 64–65.

71 Hitchens is one of the few New Atheists who does not believe in scientism, but as a materialist fails to show why.

72 Einstein, *The Expanded Quotable Einstein*, 214.

73 W. K. Clifford, *The Ethics of Belief and Other Essays* (Amherst: Prometheus Books, 1999).

74 William James, *The Will to Believe and Other Essays in Popular Philosophy*, eds. F. Burkhardt, *et al.* (Cambridge, MA: Harvard University Press, 1979).

75 To be fair to Clifford, he did argue that it was appropriate to believe things on probabilistic evidence. Still, the point

seems valid. The probability of, say, a good wife only emerges through prudent engagement and a bit of faith.

76 Obviously, they would embrace energy, wave theory, dark matter, anti-matter, and the like, but put these as expressions of the physical universe and thus under this umbrella.

77 Baggini, *Atheism*, 4–6.

78 Baggini, *Atheism*, 25–29.

79 I'm thinking of Friedrich Hayek's *The Counter-Revolution of Science: Studies in the Abuse of Reason* (1952) and the many writings of Karl Popper.

80 Baggini, *Atheism*, 25–29.

81 Edward O. Wilson, *On Human Nature* (New York: Bantam, 1978), 201.

82 As cited in John Hick, *The Existence of God* (New York: Macmillan, 1964), 170–71. The audio of this debate can be found at archive.org/details/DebateOnTheExistenceOfGod-BertrandRussellV.Fr.FrederickCopleston.

83 Dawkins, *The God Delusion*, 52.

84 Alvin Plantinga, *Warranted Christian Belief* (Oxford: Oxford University Press, 2000), 406.

85 Stephen Jay Gould, "Impeaching a Self-Appointed Judge," *Scientific American* 267, no. 1 (1992), as cited by Timothy Keller, *A Reason for God: Belief in the Age of Skepticism* (New York: Dutton, 2008), 91.

86 Alvin Plantinga, "Darwin, Mind, and Meaning," *Books and Culture* (May/June 1996).

87 As cited by Philip Yancey, "Dark Nature: The Prophets of Evolutionary Biology Want to Reduce Us to Mere Survival Machines," *Books and Culture* (March 1998).

88 Susan Blackmore, "The Power of Memes," in *Scientific American* 283, no. 4 (October 2000): 52–61.

89 Dawkins, *The God Delusion*, 231–32.

90 Robert Aunger, *Darwinizing Culture: The Status of Memetics as a Science* (New York: Oxford University Press, 2000), 7.

91 David Bentley Hart, *Atheist Delusions: The Christian Revolution and Its Fashionable Enemies* (New Haven: Yale University Press, 2009), 6–7.

92 See Jon Eccles and Karl Popper, *The Self and Its Brain* (Oxford: Routledge, 1984).

93 Matthew Alper, *The 'God' Part of the Brain: A Scientific Interpretation of Human Spirituality and God* (New York: Rogue, 2001), 127.

94 Jerry Coyne, "The Fairy Tales of Evolutionary Psychology," *The New Republic*, March 4, 2000, as cited in Beauregard and O'Leary, *The Spiritual Brain*, 11.

95 Jonah Goldberg, "Giving Thanks—and Not Just for Evolutionary Reasons," http://townhall.com/columnists/jonahgoldberg/2005/11/23/giving_thanks_-_and_not_just_for_evolutionary_reasons/page/full.

96 Francis Collins, *The Language of God: A Scientist Presents Evidence for Belief in God* (New York: Free Press, 2006), 90. Collins goes on to describe the hypotheses that RNA might be the master replicator and how these experiments have themselves failed.

97 Thomas Nagel, "The Fear of Religion," *The New Republic*, October 23, 2006, as cited by Keller, *A Reason for God*, 92.

98 Steven Jay Gould, "Darwinian Fundamentalists," *New York Review of Books*, June 12, 1997.

99 Victor Stenger, *God: The Failed Hypothesis: How Science Shows that God Does Not Exist* (Amherst: Prometheus, 2007), 164.

100 Richard Dawkins, *River Out of Eden: A Darwinian View of Life* (New York: Basic Books, 1995), 133. See also Hitchens, *God Is Not Great*, 67.

101 Michael Scriven, *Primary Philosophy* (New York: McGraw-Hill, 1966), 103, as cited in Reitan, *Is God a Delusion? Reply to Religion's Cultural Despisers* (West Sussex: Wiley-Blackwell, 2009), 76.

102 Friedrich Nietzsche, *Joyful Wisdom*, trans. Thomas Common (New York: Frederick Ungar Publishing, 1960), 167–68.

103 "The presence or absence of a creative super-intelligence is unequivocally a scientific question....The methods we should use to settle the matter...would be purely and entirely scientific methods." Dawkins, *The God Delusion*, 82–83.

104 Dawkins, *The God Delusion*, 188–89.

105 Richard Dawkins, *The Blind Watchmaker: Why the Evidence of Evolution Reveals a Universe Without Design* (New York and London: W.W. Norton & Company, 1986), 5.

106 John Eccles, *Evolution of the Brain: Creation of the Self* (London and New York: Routledge, 1989), 241. I was led to this book and many of the following resources by Beauregard and O'Leary's *The Spiritual Brain.*

107 Carl Sagan, *The Dragons of Eden: Speculations on the Nature of Human Intelligence* (New York: Random House, 1977), 221.

108 Steve Pinker, *How the Mind Works* (New York and London: W.W. Norton & Company, 1997), 83.

109 Jean-Pierre Changeux, *Neuronal Man: The Biology of Mind* (Princeton: Princeton University Press, 1997), 169.

110 Francis Crick, *Astonishing Hypothesis: The Scientific Search for the Soul* (New York: Touchstone, 1994), 3.

111 See Michael Lemonick, "Glimpses of the Mind," *Time*, July 17, 1995.

112 See John Brockman, ed., *What Is Your Dangerous Idea? Today's Leading Thinkers on the Unthinkable* (New York: Harper Perennial, 2007), 23.

113 While I will be citing Dennett directly, I am also indebted to John Symons, whose sympathetic interpretation of Dennett's work has guided me. See John Symons, *On Dennett* (Belmont: Wadsworth, 2002).

114 See Daniel Dennett, "Quining Qualia," in *Consciousness and Contemporary Science*, eds. A. J. Marcel and E. Bisiach (New York: Oxford University Press, 1988), and Daniel Dennett, "Qualia Disqualified," in *Consciousness Explained* (Boston: Little, Brown, 1991), ch. 12.

115 Bertrand Russell, *Bertrand Russell's Dictionary of Mind, Matter, and Morals* (New York: Philosophical Library, 1952), 79.

116 Peter van Inwagen's consequent argument against determinism is considered daunting by most. Part of that argument is simply that if determinism is true, then our acts are the consequences of the laws of nature and events in the remote past, which I could not affect. If I am not capable of affecting these conditions then the consequences of those things (including my present acts) are not up to me. This is just a part of the argument. Dennett tries to take on van Inwagen in his article "Who's Afraid of Determinism?: Rethinking Causes and Possibilities," in *Oxford Handbook on Free will*, ed. R. Kane (Oxford: Oxford University Press, 2002), 257–77. But it has been pointed out that he completely misreads (and then demolishes only the straw man) van Inwagen's argument. See John Martin Fischer, "Dennett on the Basic Argument," *Metaphysiology* 36 , no. 4 (July 2005): 427–35.

117 Timothy O'Connor, "Pastoral Counsel for the Anxious Naturalist: Daniel Dennett's 'Freedom Evolves,'" *Metaphysiology* 36, no. 4 (July 2005): 436–48 at 436, 444.

118 See Manuel Vargas "Compatibilism Evolves?: On Some Varieties of Dennett Worth Wanting," *Metaphysiology* 36 , no. 4 (July 2005): 460–75.

119 Dennett, *Freedom Evolves*, 307.

120 O'Connor, "Pastoral Counsel for the Anxious Naturalist," 438.

121 Plantinga, "Darwin's Dangerous Idea."

122 See B. Alan Wallace, *The Taboo of Subjectivity: Toward a New Science of Consciousness* (Oxford: Oxford University Press, 2000).

123 Nick Herbert, *Quantum Reality: Beyond the New Physics* (New York: Anchor Books, 1985), 249.

124 See, for example, Steven Weinberg's *Dreams of a Final Theory: The Scientist's Search for the Ultimate Laws of Nature* and Steven Palmer's *Vision Science: Photons to Phenomenology.*

125 Wallace, *The Taboo of Subjectivity,* 81.

126 Harris, *The End of Faith,* 191.

127 Sam Harris, *The Moral Landscape: How Science Can Determine Human Values* (New York: Free Press, 2010).

128 Dawkins, *The God Delusion,* 264–65; Hitchens, *God Is Not Great,* 266.

129 Dawkins, *The God Delusion,* 165.

130 See Sandra Menssen and Thomas Sullivan, *The Agnostic Inquirer: Revelation from a Philosophical Standpoint* (Grand Rapids: Eerdmans, 2007), 281–87.

131 See Frederick Copleston, *A History of Philosophy, Vol. VI—Modern Philosophy: From the French Enlightenment to Kant* (New York: Doubleday, 1994), 334–35.

132 See *Critique of Practical Reason,* #233, as cited in Copleston, *History of Philosophy,* 343. Direct Kant on this would be: Immanuel Kant, *Practical Philosophy,* trans. and ed. Mary J. Gregor (Cambridge: Cambridge University Press, 1996), 244.

133 See Kant's letter to Ludwig Ernst Borowski, October 24, 1792, in *Correspondence/Immanuel Kant,* trans. Arnulf Zweig (Cambridge: Cambridge University Press, 1999), 436–37.

134 I lay this out more fully in my *The Developing Christian: Spiritual Growth Through the Life Cycle* (Mahwah, NJ: Paulist Press, 2007), 41–47.

135 Dawkins, *The God Delusion*, 252–54.

136 As cited by Terence Nichols, *The Sacred Cosmos: Christian Faith and the Challenge of Naturalism* (Grand Rapids: Brazos, 2003), 15.

137 Menssen and Sullivan, *The Agnostic Inquirer*, 253.

138 Jeremy Waldron, *God, Locke, and Equality: Christian Foundations in Locke's Political Thought* (Cambridge: Cambridge University Press, 2002), 2–3, as discussed in Menssen and Sullivan, *The Agnostic Inquirer*, 257.

139 G.E.M. Anscombe, "Modern Moral Philosophy," in *The Collected Philosophical Papers of G.E.M. Anscombe*, Vol. III (Minneapolis: University of Minnesota Press, 1981), as cited in Menssen and Sullivan, 258.

140 Mark Buchanan, "Charity Begins with Homo Sapiens," *New Scientist*, March 12, 2005, as cited in Mario Beauregard and O'Leary, *The Spiritual Brain*, 9.

141 Nietzsche, 167–68.

142 Damon Linker, "Nietzsche's Truth," *First Things* 125 (August/September 2002), 59. For a fuller understanding of Nietzsche I recommend Rudiger Safranski, *Nietzsche: A Philosophical Biography* (New York: W.W. Norton & Company, 2003).

143 See Haught, "Amateur Atheists."

144 Robert Putnam and David Campbell, *American Grace: How Religion Divides and Unites Us* (New York: Simon & Schuster, 2010).

145 "Religion Does More Harm than Good—Poll," *The Guardian*, December 23, 2006, http://www.guardian.co.uk/uk/2006/dec/23/religion.topstories3.

146 In my mind, the best and fairest book on this issue is Scott Appleby's *The Ambivalence of the Sacred: Religion, Violence, and Reconciliation* (Lanham: Rowman & Littlefield, 2000). Appleby takes up the question of South Africa on pages 34–40. I also recommend Charles Selengut's *Sacred Fury: Understanding Religious Violence* (Lanham: AltaMira Press, 2003).

147 I'm counting the big ones as the American Revolution; War of 1812; War of Texas Independence; Mexican-American War; Civil War; WW I; WW II; Korea; Vietnam; Persian Gulf; Afghanistan; and Iraq. If we include smaller encounters from the pre-independence wars to such wars as the Franco-American naval war (1798–1800) or Barbary wars (1801–1805; 1815), then the list is much longer and my point that none of these conflicts involved religion is even stronger.

148 Susan Blackmore, *The Meme Machine* (Oxford: Oxford University Press, 1999), 199. Blackmore doesn't even offer an argument here, and certainly no evidence.

149 Harris, *The End of Faith*, 27.

150 Dawkins, *The God Delusion*, 335.

151 Greg Austin, Todd Kranock, and Thom Oommen, *God and War: An Audit & Explanation*, http://news.bbc.co.uk/2/shared/spl/hi/world/04/war_audit_pdf/pdf/war_audit.pdf. I was led to this by Tina Beattie, *The New Atheism: The Twilight of Reason and the War of Religion* (Maryknoll, NY: Orbis, 2007).

152 Beattie, *The New Atheism*, 78.

153 Dawkins, *The God Delusion*, 278.

154 Harris, *The End of Faith*, 79.

155 Dawkins, *The God Delusion*, 278; Harris, *The End of Faith*, 79.

156 Hitchens, *God Is Not Great*, 232.

157 Tom Pyszczynski, Sheldon Solomon, and Jeff Greenberg, *In the Wake of 9/11: The Psychology of Terror* (Washington, D.C.: American Psychological Association, 2003), 148.

158 Kofi Annan, "Secretary-General, addressing headquarters seminar on confronting Islamophobia," United Nations Press Release, December 7, 2004.

159 Harris, *Letter to a Christian Nation*, 85 (emphasis in text).

160 Harris, *The End of Faith*, 110 (emphasis in text).

161 Dawkins, 347. Here he is citing Patrick Sookhdeo approvingly.

162 Harris, *The End of Faith*, 123.

163 *Ibid.*, 110.

164 *Ibid.*, 151–52.

165 Esposito, *Who Speaks for Islam*, 73.

166 *Ibid.*, 78.

167 Interview with Scott McConnell, "The Logic of Suicide Terrorism," *The American Conservative*, July 18, 2005, as cited in Esposito, *Who Speaks for Islam*, 77.

168 Esposito, *Who Speaks for Islam*, 95.

169 Seyyed Hossein Nasr, *The Heart of Islam: Enduring Values for Humanity* (New York: HarperSanFrancisco, 2002), 266–9.

170 Esposito, *Who Speaks for Islam*?, xii–xiii, 61–62.

171 William Cavanaugh, *The Myth of Religious Violence: Secular Ideology and the Roots of Modern Conflict* (Oxford: Oxford University Press, 2010), 183.

172 Hitchens, "Bush's Secularist Triumph," *Slate*, November 9, 2004, http://www.slate.com/articles/news_and_politics/fighting_words/2004/11/bushs_secularist_triumph.html.

173 Harris, *The End of Faith*, 128–129.

174 Cavanaugh, *The Myth of Religious Violence*, 228.

175 Armstrong, *A Case for God*, xv.

176 Rumi, *The Essential Rumi*, trans. Coleman Banks (New York: HarperSanFrancisco, 1995), 32.

177 Armstrong, *A Case for God*, xii-xiii.

178 Leszek Kolakowski, *Religion* (South Bend: St. Augustine's Press, 2001), 165.

179 Harris, *The End of Faith*, 15.

180 *Ibid.*, 13.

181 Francis X. Clooney, "Theology, Dialogue, and Religious Others: Some Recent Books in the Theology of Religions and Related Fields," *Religious Studies Review* 29 (2003): 319.

182 Dawkins, *The God Delusion*, 268–316.

183 Harris, *The End of Faith*, 8.

184 Hitchens, *God Is Not Great*, 115, 217.

185 Matthew 5:3–10.

186 Helga Kuhse, "Introduction," in Peter Singer, *Unsanctifying Human Life: Essays on Ethics* (Oxford: Blackwell, 2002), 11.

187 Hitchens, *God Is Not Great*, 221.

188 Dawkins, *The Blind Watchmaker*, 5.

189 Dawkins, *The God Delusion*, 403 (emphasis in original).

190 Second Vatican Council, *Gaudiem et Spes: Pastoral Constitution on the Church*, no. 39, http://www.vatican.va/archive/hist_councils/ii_vatican_council/documents/vat-ii_cons_19651207_gaudium-et-spes_en.html.

191 This is discussed quite well in Haught, *God and the New Atheism*, 82–83.

192 Patricia S. Churchland, "Epistemology in an Age of Neuroscience," *Journal of Philosophy* 84, no. 10 (1987): 548.

193 Richard Dawkins, *River out of Eden* (New York: Basic Books, 1995), 133.

194 Harris, *The End of Faith*, 13.

195 Pope John Paul II, "The Meaning of the Assisi Day of Prayer," *Origins*, 16, no. 31 (1987), 562.

196 Sagan, "The God Hypothesis," in *The Portable Atheist*, 238.

197 Harris, *The End of Faith*, 19.

198 Alvin Plantinga, "A Christian Life Partly Lived," in *Philosophers Who Believe: The Spiritual Journeys of 11 Leading Thinkers*, ed. Kelly James Clark (Downers Grove: InterVarsity Press, 1993).

199 C.S. Lewis, *Mere Christianity* (New York: Macmillan, 1960), 31, as cited by Keller, *The Reason for God*, 26.

200 Richard Swinburne, *The Existence of God*, 2nd ed. (Oxford: Clarendon, 2004), 264.

201 Clara Claiborne Park, *The Siege: The First Eight Years With an Autistic Child, With an Epilogue Fifteen Years Later* (Boston: Little, Brown 2002), 320.

202 Both as cited in Keller, *A Reason for God*, 33–34.

203 Czeslaw Milosz, "The Discreet Charms of Nihilism," *New York Review of Books*, November 19, 1998, as cited by Keller, *A Reason for God*, 75.

204 This essay is reprinted in Hitchens, *The Portable Atheist*, 32–45.

205 John Polkinghorne, *Science and Theology—An Introduction* (Minneapolis: Fortress Press, 1998), 93.

206 See, for example, Lisa Schwebel, *Apparitions, Healings, and Weeping Madonnas* (New York: Paulist Press, 2004).

207 Shimon Malin, *Nature Loves to Hide: Quantum Physics and the Nature of Reality, a Western Perspective* by Shimon Malin (Oxford: Oxford University Press, 2001), 143.

208 *Ibid.*, 226.

209 *Ibid.*

210 *Ibid.*, 176.

211 Alexis Carrel, *The Voyage to Lourdes* (New York: Harper & Brothers, 1959), 22, as cited by Nichols, *The Sacred Cosmos*, 187.

212 P.G. Boissarie, *Healing at Lourdes* (Baltimore: John Murphy), 197–9, as cited in Nichols, *The Sacred Cosmos*, 187.

213 Boissarie, *Healing at Lourdes*, 2–9, as cited by Nichols, *The Sacred Cosmos*, 188.

214 *Ibid.*

215 Crick, *The Astonishing Hypothesis*, 3.

216 Alan Turing, "Computing Machinery and Intelligence," *Mind* 59, no. 236 (1950), in *The Mind's I: Fantasies and Reflections on Self and Soul*, eds. Douglas Hofstadter and Daniel Dennett (New York: Basic Books, 1981), 66.

217 Beauregard and O'Leary, *The Spiritual Brain*, 170–71.

218 *Ibid.*, 171.

219 See Nichols, *The Sacred Cosmos*, 161–62. For much of the following material I am heavily reliant on Nichols, *Death and Afterlife: A Theological Introduction* (Grand Rapids, Brazos, 2010), 92–110. Nichols and I were for many years colleagues and have shared and taught this information, including materials drawn on here.

220 Elisabeth Kübler-Ross, *On Children and Death* (New York: Macmillian/Collier, 1983), 207–11, as cited in Nichols, *The Sacred Cosmos*, 161–62.

221 These include Dr. Michael Sabom's thirty-two case studies and Dr. Pim van Lommel's sixty-two case studies. See Nichols, *Death and Afterlife*, 94–95.

222 *Ibid.*

223 See http://www.laphamsquarterly.org/roundtable/roundtable/an-atheist-meets-the-masters-of-the-universe.php.

224 Dawkins, *The God Delusion*, 131.

225 Blaise Pascal, *Pensées*, revised ed., trans. Alban Krailsheimer (New York: Penguin, 1995), no. 449.

226 I am reliant in this section on Thomas Morris, *Making Sense of It All: Pascal and the Meaning of Life* (Grand Rapids, Eerdmans, 1991).

227 Pascal, *Pensées*, no. 418.

228 *Ibid.*, no. 427.

229 *Ibid.*, no. 418.

230 Morris, *Making Sense of It All*, 124.

231 Pascal, *Pensées*, no. 417.

232 *Ibid.*, no. 418.

233 Cottingham, *The Spiritual Dimension*, 8.

234 The best expression of this is Plantinga's *Warranted Christian Belief, passim*, where Plantinga lays out the noetic qualities of the psyche and how transcendental knowledge might be recognized by it, how toxic qualities of the mind block its proper function, and how the mind might become available to the divine again.

235 Cottingham, *Why Believe?*, 59–62.

236 See John Boslough, *Stephen Hawking's Universe*, (New York: William Morrow, 1985), 121.

237 Stephen Hawking, *A Brief History of Time*, 10th ed. (New York: Bantam, 1988), 131.

238 For most of the following material, I am utterly indebted to and freely drawing on Robert Spitzer, *New Proofs for the Existence of God: Contributions of Contemporary Physics and Philosophy* (Grand Rapids, MI: Eerdmans, 2010).

239 I am not going to address the theory that Dawkins brings up by Lee Smolin, who argued that black holes can produce baby universes. Dawkins concedes that "not all physicists are enthusiastic about Smolin's scenario." Actually, none are any

more. Hawking imagined that these were theoretically possible, and would be conceivably like black holes being portals or wormholes through which bubbles of false vacuum energy could tunnel to spawn a new expanding universe. This was the subject of a famous bet he had with James Preskill. In 2006, he conceded, "There is no baby universe branching off....I'm sorry to disappoint science fiction fans...." This paper can be accessed through Cornell University, http://arxiv.org/abs/hepth/0507171.

240 Alex Vilenkin, *Many Worlds in One: The Search for Other Universes* (New York: Hill and Wang, 2006), 175, as cited in William Lane Craig and Chad Meister, eds., *God Is Great, God Is Good: Why Believing in God Is Reasonable and Responsible* (Downers Grove: InterVarsity Press, 2009), 16.

241 Antony Flew, *There Is a God: How the World's Most Notorious Atheist Changed His Mind* (New York: Harper One, 2007), 124.

242 William Schweiker, "The Varieties and Revisions of Atheism," *Zygon* 40, no. 2 (2005): 270.

243 Spitzer, *Proofs for God*, 50.

244 Paul Davies, *God and the New Physics* (New York: Touchstone, 1984), 189. I was originally led to this work by Spitzer's *Proofs for God*.

245 As cited in Spitzer, *Proofs for God*, 59.

246 Francis Collins in Salon.com, http://www.salon.com/books/int/2006/08/07/collins/index2.html.

247 Dawkins, *The God Delusion*, 167–75.

248 Plantinga, "Dennett's Dangerous Idea." This is my gloss.

249 Bruce L. Gordon, "Inflationary Cosmology and the String Multiverse," in Spitzer, *Proofs for God*, 103.

Bibliography

Adams, Marilyn McCord. *Horrendous Evils and the Goodness of God.* Ithaca: Cornell University Press, 1999.

Ahlstrom, Sydney. *A Religious History of the American People.* Garden City: Image Books, 1975.

Ahmad, Aijaz. "Islam, Islamisms, and the West." *The Socialist Register* 44 (2008). http://socialistregister.com/index.php/srv/article/view/5873#.UnRvChDIv3A.

Aunger, Robert. *Darwinizing Culture: The Status of Memetics as a Science.* New York: Oxford University Press, 2000.

Alper, Matthew. *The 'God' Part of the Brain: A Scientific Interpretation of Human Spirituality and God.* New York: Rogue, 2001.

Alter, Torin, and Sven Walter. *Phenomenal Concepts and Phenomenal Knowledge: New Essays on Consciousness and Physicalism.* Oxford: Oxford University Press, 2007.

Anscombe, G.E.M., "Modern Moral Philosophy," in *The Collected Philosophical Papers of G.E.M. Anscombe*, Vol. III. Minneapolis: University of Minnesota Press, 1981.

Antoun, Richard. *Understanding Fundamentalism: Christian, Islamic, and Jewish Movements*, 2nd ed. Lanham: Rowman & Littlefield, 2008.

Appleby, Scott. *The Ambivalence of the Sacred: Religion, Violence, and Reconciliation.* Lanham: Rowman & Littlefield, 2000.

Armstrong, Karen. *A Case for God*. New York and Toronto: Alfred A. Knopf, 2009.

Atkins, Peter. *Creation Revisited*. Oxford and New York: W.H. Freeman, 1992.

Baggini, Julian. *Atheism: A Very Short Introduction*. Oxford: Oxford University Press, 2003.

Barbour, Ian. *Religion and Science*. San Francisco: Harper, 1997.

Barbour, Ian. *When Science Meets Religion*. New York: HarperCollins, 2000.

Barrow, John, and Frank Tipler. *The Anthropic Cosmological Principle*. Oxford and New York: Oxford University Press, 1986.

Beattie, Tina. *The New Atheism: The Twilight of Reason and the War on Religion*. Maryknoll: Orbis, 2007.

Beauregard, Mario, and Denyse O'Leary. *The Spiritual Brain: A Neuroscientist's Case for the Existence of the Soul*. New York: HarperOne, 2007.

Beckwith, Francis. "Dawkins, God, and the Scientific Enterprise: Reflections on the Appeal to Darwinism in Fundamentalist Atheism." In *Intelligent Design: William A. Dembski and Michael Ruse in Dialogue*, edited by Robert Stewart, 101–11. Minneapolis: Fortress Press, 2007.

Behe, Michael. *Darwin's Black Box: The Biochemical Challenge to Evolution*. New York: Free Press, 1996.

Bennett, M.R., and P.M.S. Hacker. *Philosophical Foundations of Neuroscience*. Malden: Blackwell, 2003.

Berger, Peter. *The Rumor of Angels: Modern Society and the Rediscovery of the Supernatural*. New York: Doubleday, 1970.

Billington, Ray. *Religion Without God*. London and New York: Routledge, 2002.

Blackmore, Susan. "The Power of Memes." *Scientific American* 283, no. 4 (2000): 52–61.

Blackmore, Susan. *The Meme Machine*. Oxford and New York: Oxford University Press, 1999.

Blanshard, Brand. *Reason and Belief.* New Haven: Yale University Press, 1974.

Boyer, Pascal. *Religion Explained: The Evolutionary Origins of Religious Thought*. New York: Basic Books, 2000.

Brockman, John. *The Third Culture*. New York: Touchstone Books, 1996.

Brook, Andrew, and Don Ross, eds. *Daniel Dennett*. Cambridge: Cambridge University Press, 2002.

Buckley, Michael J. "The Madman and the Crowd: For the New Atheists, God Is Not Worth a Decent Argument." *America* 198, no. 15 (2008): 27–29.

Buckley, Michael J. *At the Origins of Modern Atheism*. New Haven and London: Yale University Press, 1987.

Buckley, Michael J. *Denying and Disclosing God: The Ambiguous Progress of Modern Atheism*. New Haven and London: Yale University Press, 2004.

Burch, Sharon Peebles. "On Atheism: A Response to Ted Peters." *Dialog: A Journal of Theology* 46, no. 4 (2007): 390–93.

Cavanaugh, William. *The Myth of Religious Violence: Secular Ideology and the Roots of Modern Conflict*. Oxford: Oxford University Press, 2010.

Chabris, Christopher, and Daniel Simons. *The Invisible Gorilla: And Other Ways Our Intuitions Deceive Us*. New York: Crown, 2010.

Clifford, W.K. *The Ethics of Belief and Other Essays*. Amherst: Prometheus Books, 1999.

Clooney, Francis X. "Theology, Dialogue, and Religious Others: Some Recent Books in the Theology of Religions and Related Fields." *Religious Studies Review* 29 (2003): 319–27.

Collins, Francis. *The Language of God: A Scientist Presents Evidence for Belief in God.* New York: Free Press, 2006.

Cooper, Terry. *Dimensions of Evil: Contemporary Perspectives.* Minneapolis: Fortress Press, 2007.

Cottingham, John. *Why Believe?* New York: Continuum, 2009.

Cottingham, John. *The Spiritual Dimension: Religion, Philosophy, and Human Value.* Cambridge: Cambridge University Press, 2005.

Craig, William Lane, and Chad Meister, eds. *God Is Great, God Is Good: Why Believing in God Is Reasonable and Responsible.* Downers Grove, IL: InterVarsity Press, 2009.

Craig, William Lane, and Quentin Smith. *Theism, Atheism, and Big Bang Cosmology.* Oxford: Clarendon Press, 1993.

Craig, William Lane. "God Is Not Dead Yet: How Current Philosophers Argue for His Existence." *Christianity Today* 52, no. 7 (2008): 22–27.

Crick, Francis. *The Astonishing Hypothesis: The Scientific Search for the Soul.* New York: Touchstone, 1994.

D'Aquili, Eugene, and Andrew B. Newberg. *The Mystical Mind: Probing the Biology of Religious Experience.* Minneapolis: Fortress Press, 1999.

D'Souza, Dinesh. *What's So Great About Christianity.* Washington, D.C.: Regnery Publishing, 2007.

Dahlbom, Bo, ed. *Dennett and His Critics: Demystifying Mind.* Oxford, UK and Cambridge, USA: Blackwell, 1993.

Dawkins, Richard. *River Out of Eden: A Darwinian View of Life.* New York: Basic Books, 1995.

Dawkins, Richard. *The Ancestor's Tale: A Pilgrimage to the Dawn of Evolution.* Boston and New York: Houghton Mifflin Company, 2004.

Dawkins, Richard. *The Blind Watchmaker: Why the Evidence of Evolution Reveals a Universe Without Design.* New York and London: W.W. Norton & Company, 1986.

Dawkins, Richard. *The God Delusion.* 2nd ed. New York: Mariner Books, 2008.

Dawkins, Richard. *The Oxford Book of Modern Science Writing.* Oxford: Oxford University Press, 2008.

Dawkins, Richard. *The Selfish Gene.* 2nd ed. Oxford: Oxford University Press, 1989.

Dawkins, Richard. *Unweaving the Rainbow: Science, Delusion, and the Appetite for Wonder.* Boston and New York: Houghton Mifflin Company, 1998.

Dehaene, Stanislas. *The Cognitive Neuroscience of Consciousness.* Amsterdam: Elsevier Science Publishers, 2001.

Dembski, William, and James Kushner, eds. *Signs of Intelligence: Understanding Intelligent Design.* Grand Rapids: Brazos, 2001.

Dennett, Daniel. *Breaking the Spell: Religion as a Natural Phenomenon.* New York: Viking, 2006.

Dennett, Daniel. *Consciousness Explained.* Boston: Little, Brown, 1991.

Dennett, Daniel. *Darwin's Dangerous Idea: Evolution and the Meaning of Life.* New York: Simon & Schuster, 1995.

Dennett, Daniel. *Elbow Room: The Varieties of Free Will Worth Wanting.* Cambridge, Mass: MIT Press, 1984.

Dennett, Daniel. *Freedom Evolves.* New York: Penguin, 2003.

Dennett, Daniel. *Sweet Dreams: Philosophical Obstacles to a Science of Consciousness.* Cambridge: MIT Press, 2005.

Dennett, Daniel. *The Intentional Stance.* Cambridge: MIT Press, 1987.

Eagleton, Terry. *Reason, Faith, and Revelation: Reflections on the God Debate.* New Haven and London: Yale University Press, 2009.

Eagleton, Terry. "Lunging, Flailing, Mispunching: A Review of Richard Dawkins' 'The God Delusion.'" *London Review of Books*, October 19, 2006.

Eccles, John C. *Evolution of the Brain: Creation of the Self.* London and New York: Routledge, 1989.

Eccles, John C., and Karl Popper. *The Self and Its Brain.* Oxford: Routledge, 1984.

Einstein, Albert. *Albert Einstein: The Human Side.* Edited by Helen Dukas and Banesh Hoffmann. Princeton: Princeton University Press, 1979.

Einstein, Albert. *The Expanded Quotable Einstein.* Princeton: Princeton University Press, 2000.

Esposito, John L., and Dalia Mogahed. *Who Speaks for Islam: What a Billion Muslims Really Think.* New York: Gallup Press, 2007.

Feldmeier, Peter. *Encountering Faith: Christianity in Interreligious Dialogue.* Winona: Anselm Academic, 2011.

Feldmeier, Peter. *The Developing Christian: Spiritual Growth Through the Life Cycle.* Mahwah: Paulist Press, 2007.

Fischer, John Martin. "Dennett on the Basic Argument." *Metaphysiology* 36, no. 4 (2005): 427–35.

Flew, Antony, and Roy Abraham Varghese. *There Is a God: How the World's Most Notorious Atheist Changed His Mind.* New York: HarperOne, 2007.

Flew, Antony. "A Reply to Richard Dawkins." *First Things* 188 (December 2008): 21–22.

Freeman, Charles. *The Closing of the Western Mind: The Rise of Faith and the Fall of Reason.* New York: Vintage, 2002.

Freud, Sigmund. *Civilization and Its Discontents.* Translated by James Stachey. W.W. Norton & Company: New York, 1961.

Gaillardetz, Richard. "Catholicism and the New Atheism." *America* 198, no. 15 (2008): 12–15.

Gallup, George H., Jr. "Dogma Bites Man: On the New and Biased Research Linking Faith and Social Ills." *Touchstone*, December 2005.

Giberson, Karl, and Mariano Artigas. *Oracles of Science: Celebrity Scientists Versus God and Religion*. Oxford: Oxford University Press, 2007.

Giberson, Karl. *Saving Darwin: How to Be a Christian and Believe in Evolution*. New York: HarperCollins, 2008.

Gingerich, Owen. *God's Universe*. Cambridge: Belknap Press, 2006.

Gordon, Dennis. "Richard Dawkins and the God Controversy." *Stimulus* 16, no. 2 (2008): 2–5.

Gould, Stephen Jay. "Darwinian Fundamentalists." *New York Review of Books*, June 12, 1997.

Gould, Stephen Jay. *Rocks of Ages: Science and Religion in the Fullness of Life*. New York: Ballantine Publishing Group, 1999.

Granqvist, Pehr, et al., "Sensed Presence and Mystical Experiences Are Predicted by Suggestibility, Not by the Application of Transcranial Weak Complex Magnetic Fields." *Neuroscience Letters*, doi:10.1016/j.neulet.2004.10.057 (2004).

Guth, Alan. *The Inflationary Universe*. Reading: Addison-Wesley, 1997.

Guthrie, Stan. "Answering the Atheists: A Reader's Digest Version of Why I Am a Christian." *Christianity Today* 51, no. 11 (2007): 74.

Hahn, Scott, and Benjamin Wiker. *Answering the New Atheism: Dismantling Dawkins' Case Against God*. Emmaus Road: Steubenville, 2008.

Hamer, Dean. *The God Gene: How Faith Is Hardwired Into Our Genes*. New York: Doubleday, 2004.

Harbour, Daniel. *An Intelligent Person's Guide to Atheism.* London: Duckworth Publishers, 2001.

Harris, Sam. *Letter to a Christian Nation.* New York: Alfred A. Knopf, 2006.

Harris, Sam. *The End of Faith: Religion, Terror, and the Future of Reason.* New York and London: W.W. Norton & Company, 2004.

Hart, David Bentley. *Atheist Delusions: The Christian Revolution and Its Fashionable Enemies.* New Haven and London: Yale University Press, 2009.

Harvey, Andrew, ed. *The Essential Mystics: The Soul's Journey Into Truth.* Edison: Castle Books, 1998.

Haught, John. *God and the New Atheism: A Critical Response to Dawkins, Harris, and Hitchens.* Louisville: Westminster John Knox, 2008.

Haught, John. "Amateur Atheists: Why the New Atheism Isn't Serious." *Christian Century,* February 26, 2008.

Haught, John. "True Believers: Have the New Atheists Adopted a Faith of Their Own?" *America* 198, no. 15 (2008): 16–8.

Hefner, Philip. "Modern and Postmodern Forms of Unbelief." *Christian Century* 117, no. 3(2000): 88–90.

Heschel, Abraham Joshua. *The Sabbath.* New York: Farrar, Straus, and Giroux, 1951.

Hick, John. *The Existence of God.* New York: Macmillan, 1964.

Hitchcock, S.C. *Disbelief 101: A Young Person's Guide to Atheism.* Tuscan: See Sharp Press, 2009.

Hitchens, Christopher, ed. *The Portable Atheist: Essential Readings for the Nonbeliever.* Philadelphia: Da Capo Press, 2007.

Hitchens, Christopher. *God Is Not Great: How Religion Poisons Everything.* New York: Twelve, 2007.

Hitchens, Christopher. *The Missionary Position: Mother Teresa in Theory and Practice.* London and New York: Verso, 1995.

Hofstadter, Douglas R., and Daniel Dennett. *The Mind's I: Fantasies and Reflections on Self and Soul.* New York: Basic Books, 1981.

Holder, Rodney D. *God, the Multiverse, and Everything: Modern Cosmology and the Argument from Design.* Aldershot: Ashgate, 2004.

Honderich, Ted C., ed. *The Oxford Companion to Philosophy.* Oxford: Oxford University Press, 1995.

Hunter, Michael, and David Wootton, eds. *Atheism From the Reformation to the Enlightenment.* Oxford: Clarendon Press, 1992.

Hyman, Lawrence. "Whatever Happened to Atheism?" *Skeptic* 5, no. 2 (1997): 70.

Idel, Moshe, and Bernard McGinn, eds. *Mystical Union in Judaism, Christianity and Islam: An Ecumenical Dialogue.* New York: Continuum, 1996.

James, William. *The Will to Believe and Other Essays in Popular Philosophy.* Edited by F. Burkhardt, et al. Cambridge: Harvard University Press, 1979.

Jastrow, Robert. *God and the Astronomers.* New York: W.W. Norton & Company, 1992.

John Paul II. "The Meaning of the Assisi Day of Prayer." *Origins* 16, no. 31 (1987): 561–63.

Johnson, Luke Timothy. "Dry Bones: Why Religion Cannot Live Without Mysticism." *Commonweal*, February 26, 2010.

Joshi, S.T., ed. *Atheism: A Reader.* Amherst: Prometheus Books, 2000.

Kane, Robert, ed. *The Oxford Handbook of Free Will.* Oxford: Oxford University Press, 2002.

Kant, Immanuel. *Critique of Practical Reason*. Edited by Mary Gregor. Cambridge: Cambridge University Press, 1997.

Kay, James. "Christian Atheism?" *Theology Today* 65, no. 2 (July 2008): 139–43.

Keller, Timothy. *The Reason for God: Belief in the Age of Skepticism*. New York: Dutton, 2008.

Klostermaier, Klaus. "Reflections Prompted by Richard Dawkins' 'The God Delusion.'" *Journal of Ecumenical Studies* 43, no. 4 (2008).

Knitter, Paul. *Introducing Theologies of Religion*. Maryknoll: Orbis, 2002.

Kolakowski, Leszek. *Religion: If There Is No God*. South Bend: St. Augustine's Press, 1983.

Krueger, Douglas E. *What Is Atheism?: A Short Introduction*. Amherst: Prometheus Books, 1998.

Lewontin, Richard. "Billions and Billions of Demons." *The New York Review of Books* 44, no. 1 (January 1997).

Linker, Damon. "Nietzsche's Truth." *First Things* 125 (August/September 2002): 50–60.

Lochman, Jan Milic. "Christ and/or Prometheus: Theological Issues in the Encounter Between Christians and Marxists." *Journal of Ecumenical Studies* 22, no. 3 (1985): 440–53.

Mackie, John. *The Miracle of Theism: Arguments for and Against the Existence of God*. Oxford: Clarendon Press, 1982.

Malin, Shimon. *Nature Loves to Hide: Quantum Physics and the Nature of Reality, a Western Perspective*. Oxford: Oxford University Press, 2001.

Marcel, A., and E. Bisiach, *Consciousness and Contemporary Science*. New York: Oxford University Press, 1988.

Margulis, Lynn, and Eduardo Punset, eds. *Mind, Life, and the Universe: Conversations with Great Scientists of Our Time.* White River Junction: Chelsea Green Publishing Company, 2007.

Markham, Ian S. *Against Atheism: Why Dawkins, Hitchens, and Harris Are Fundamentally Wrong.* West Sussex: Wiley-Blackwell, 2010.

Martin, Michael, ed. *The Cambridge Companion to Atheism.* Cambridge: Cambridge University Press, 2007.

McCarthy, Joan. *Dennett and Ricoeur on the Narrative Self.* Amherst: Humanity Books, 2007.

McGrath, Alister. *The Order of Things: Explorations in Scientific Theology.* Malden: Blackwell, 2006.

McGrath, Alister, and Joanna Collicutt McGrath. *The Dawkins Delusion? Atheist Fundamentalism and the Denial of the Divine.* Downers Grove: InterVarsity Press, 2007.

McGrath, Alister. "Has Science Eliminated God?—Richard Dawkins and the Meaning of Life." *Science and Christian Belief* 17, no. 2 (2005): 115–35.

McGrath, Alister. "The Twilight of Atheism." *Christianity Today* 49, no. 3 (March 2005): 36–40.

McGrath, Alister. *The Reenchantment of Nature: The Denial of Religion and the Ecological Crisis.* New York: Doubleday, 2002.

McGrath, Alister. *The Twilight of Atheism: The Rise and Fall of Disbelief in the Modern World.* New York: Doubleday, 2004.

McGrath, Alister. *Dawkins' God: Genes, Memes, and the Meaning of Life.* Malden: Blackwell, 2005.

McMichael, Ralph N., Jr. *Walter Kasper's Response to Modern Atheism: Confessing the Trinity.* New York: Peter Lang, 2006.

Mele, Alfred. "Dennett on Freedom." *Metaphysiology* 36, no. 4 (July 2005): 414–26.

Menon, Latha, ed. *A Devil's Chaplain: Selected Essays by Richard Dawkins.* London: Weidenfeld & Nicolson, 2003.

Menssen, Sandra, and Thomas D. Sullivan. *The Agnostic Inquirer: Revelation From a Philosophical Standpoint.* Grand Rapids: Eerdmans, 2007.

Miller, Kenneth. *Finding Darwin's God: A Scientist's Search for Common Ground Between God and Evolution.* New York: Perennial, 1999.

Mittleman, Alan. "Asking the Wrong Question." *First Things* 189 (January 2009): 15–17.

Mohler, R. Albert, Jr. *Atheism Remix: A Christian Confronts the New Atheism.* Wheaton: Crossway Books, 2008.

Moreman, Christopher. *Beyond the Threshold: Afterlife Beliefs and Experiences in World Religions.* Plymouth: Rowman & Littlefield, 2008.

Morey, Robert A. *The New Atheism and the Erosion of Freedom.* Minneapolis: Bethany House, 1986.

Morris, Thomas V. *Making Sense of It All: Pascal and the Meaning of Life.* Grand Rapids: Eerdmans, 1991.

Mouw, Richard. "An Evangelical Moment? To Combat the Rise of Atheism, Christians Must First Look to Themselves." *America* 198, no. 15 (May 5, 2008): 20–22.

Nagel, Thomas, *The Last Word.* New York and Oxford: Oxford University Press, 1997.

Nasr, Seyyed Hossein. *Islamic Spirituality: Foundations.* New York: Crossroad, 1987.

Nietzsche, Friedrich. *Joyful Wisdom.* Translated by Thomas Common. New York: Frederick Ungar Publishing, 1960.

Newberg, Andrew, Eugene D'Aquili, and Vince Rause. *Why God Won't Go Away: Brain Science and the Biology of Belief.* New York: Ballantine Books, 2001.

Newberg, Andrew, and Eugene D'Aquili. *The Mystical Mind: Probing the Biology of Religious Experience.* Minneapolis: Fortress Press, 1999.

Nichols, Terence. *The Sacred Cosmos: Christian Faith and the Challenge of Naturalism.* Grand Rapids: Brazos, 2003.

Nichols, Terence. "Understanding the Creator from the Things that Are Made." *Logos* 13, no. 4 (Fall 2010): 155–74.

Nichols, Terence. *Death and Afterlife: A Theological Introduction.* Grand Rapids, Brazos, 2010

Novak, Michael. *No One Sees God: Dark Night of Atheists and Believers.* New York: Doubleday, 2008.

O'Connor, Timothy, ed. *Agents, Causes, Events: Essays on Indeterminism and Free Will.* New York and Oxford: Oxford University Press, 1995.

O'Connor, Timothy. "Pastoral Counsel for the Anxious Naturalist: Daniel Dennett's 'Freedom Evolves.'" *Metaphysiology* 36, no. 4 (July 2005): 436–48.

Opocensky, Milan. "Atheism—A Radical Humanism?" *Journal of Ecumenical Studies* 22 (1985): 516–19.

Origen. *Origen: An Exhortation to Martyrdom, Prayer, and Selected Works.* Translated by Rowan Green. Mahwah: Paulist Press, 1981.

Padgett, Alan. "On Atheism, Pluralism, and Science: A Response to Ted Peters." *Dialog: A Journal of Theology* 46, no. (2007): 394–96.

Palmer, Stephen. *Vision Science: Photons to Phenomenology.* Cambridge: MIT Press, 1999.

Pape, Robert. *Dying to Win: The Strategic Logic of Suicide Terrorism.* New York: Random House, 2005.

Peters, Ted. "Christian God-Talk While Listening to Atheists, Pluralists, and Muslims." *Dialog: A Journal of Theology* 46, no. 2 (2007): 84–103.

Peters, Ted. "Theologians and Other Idiots." *Dialog: A Journal of Theology* 46, no. 3 (2007): 185–88.

Peterson, Gregory. "Why the New Atheism Shouldn't Be (Completely) Dismissed." *Zygon* 42, no. 4 (2007): 803–06.

Pinker, Steven. *The Blank Slate: The Modern Denial of Human Nature.* New York: Penguin, 2002.

Pinker, Steven. *How the Mind Works.* New York and London: W.W. Norton & Company, 1997.

Plantinga, Alvin. *Warrant and Proper Function.* New York and Oxford: Oxford University Press, 1993.

Plantinga, Alvin. *Warrant: The Current Debate.* New York and Oxford: Oxford University Press, 1993.

Plantinga, Alvin. *Warranted Christian Belief.* New York and Oxford: Oxford University Press, 2000.

Plantinga, Alvin. "Darwin's Dangerous Idea: Evolution and the Meanings of Life." *Books and Culture* 2 (May/June 1996): 16–18.

Polkinghorne, John. *Science and Theology—An Introduction.* Minneapolis, Fortress Press, 1998.

Poole, M. "A Critique of Aspects of the Philosophy and Theology of Richard Dawkins." *Science & Christian Belief* 6, no. 1 (1994): 41–59.

Pope, Steven. "Called to Love: Christian Witness Can Be the Best Response to Atheist Polemics." *America* 198, no. 15 (2008): 23–26.

Prothero, Stephen. *Religious Literacy: What Every American Needs to Know—and Doesn't.* New York: HarperOne, 2007.

Putnam, Robert, and David Campbell. *American Grace: How Religion Divides and Unites Us.* New York: Simon & Schuster, 2010.

Pyszczynski, Tom, Sheldon Solomon, and Jeff Greenberg. *In the Wake of 9/11: The Psychology of Terror.* Washington, D.C.: American Psychological Association, 2003.

Rahner, Karl. *Foundations of Christian Faith: An Introduction to the Idea of Christianity.* Translated by William Dych. New York: Crossroad, 1985.

Reitan, Eric. *Is God a Delusion? Reply to Religion's Cultural Despisers.* West Sussex: Wiley-Blackwell, 2009.

Richmond, Patrick. "Richard Dawkins' Darwinian Objection to Unexplained Complexity in God." *Science and Christian Belief* 19, no. 2 (2007): 99–116.

Robinson, Marilynne. *Absence of Mind: The Dispelling of Inwardness from the Modern Myth of the Self.* New Haven: Yale University Press, 2010.

Rumi. *The Essential Rumi.* Translated by Coleman Barks. New York: HarperSanFrancisco, 1995.

Russell, Bertrand. *Bertrand Russell's Dictionary of Mind, Matter, and Morals.* New York: Philosophical Library, 1952.

Russell, Paul. *The Riddle of Hume's "Treatise": Skepticism, Naturalism, and Irreligion.* Oxford and New York: Oxford University Press, 2008.

Sabom, Michael. *Recollections of Death: A Medical Investigation.* New York: Harper & Row, 1982.

Sagan, Carl. *The Dragons of Eden: Speculations on the Nature of Human Intelligence* (New York: Random House), 1977.

Schwartz, Jeffrey M., and Sharon Begley. *The Mind and the Brain: Neuroplasticity and the Power of Mental Force.* New York: Harper, 2002.

Schweiker, William. "The Varieties and Revisions of Atheism." *Zygon* 40, no. 2 (2005): 267–76.

Searle, John. *The Rediscovery of the Mind.* Cambridge: MIT Press, 1994.

Selengut, Charles. *Sacred Fury: Understanding Religious Violence.* Lanham: Rowman & Littlefield, 2003.

Shermer, Michael. "Do You Believe in God?: The Difference in Your Answer & the Difference It Makes." *Skeptic* 6, no. 2 (1998): 74–79.

Smart, J.J.C., and J.J. Haldane. *Atheism and Theism.* 2nd ed. Malden: Blackwell, 2003.

Smith, Christian, and Melinda Lundquist Denton. *Soul Searching: The Religious and Spiritual Lives of American Teenagers.* Oxford: Oxford University Press, 2004.

Smith, George. *The Case Against God.* Amherst: Prometheus Books, 1989.

Smolin, Lee. *Three Roads to Quantum Gravity.* New York: Basic Books, 2003.

Snow, Tony. "New Atheists Are Not Great." *Christian Century,* March 13, 2008.

Spitzer, Robert. *New Proofs for the Existence of God: Contributions of Contemporary Physics and Philosophy.* Grand Rapids: Eerdmans, 2010.

Sponheim, Paul. "The Quest for God Beyond Belief." *Word & World* 7, no. 2 (1987): 131–40.

Steele, David Ramsay, *Atheism Explained: From Folly to Philosophy.* Chicago and La Salle: Open Court, 2008.

Stenger, Victor. *God and the Folly of Faith: The Incompatibility of Science and Religion.* Amherst: Prometheus Books, 2012.

Stenger, Victor. *God: The Failed Hypothesis: How Science Shows that God Does Not Exist.* Amherst: Prometheus, 2007.

Stenger, Victor. *The New Atheism: Taking a Stand for Science and Reason.* Amherst: Prometheus Books, 2009.

Steward, Robert B., ed. *The Future of Atheism: Alister McGrath and Daniel Dennett in Dialogue.* Minneapolis: Fortress Press, 2008.

Swinburne, Richard. *The Existence of God.* 2nd ed. Oxford: Clarendon Press, 2004.

Swinburne, Richard. *The Resurrection of God.* Oxford: Clarendon Press, 2003.

Symons, John. *On Dennett.* Belmont: Wadsworth, 2002.

Thrower, James. *Western Atheism: A Short History.* Amherst: Prometheus Books, 2000.

Tipler, Frank. *The Physics of Immortality.* New York: Anchor Books, 1994.

Turner, Denys. "On Denying the Right God: Aquinas on Theism and Idolatry." *Modern Theology* 20, no. 1 (2004): 141–61.

Turner, Denys. *How to Be an Atheist.* Cambridge: Cambridge University Press, 2002.

Underhill, Evelyn. *Mysticism.* Mineola: Dover, 2002.

Van Inwagen, Peter. *An Essay of Free Will.* Oxford: Clarendon Press, 1983.

Vargas, Manuel. "Compatibilism Evolves?: On Some Varieties of Dennett Worth Wanting." *Metaphysiology* 36, no. 4 (July 2005): 460–75.

Wainwright, William J. *Reason and the Heart: A Prolegomenon to a Critique of Passional Reason.* Ithaca: Cornell University Press, 1995.

Waldman, Steven. *Founding Faith: How Our Founding Fathers Forged a Radical New Approach to Religious Liberty.* New York: Random House, 2008.

Weinberg, Steven. *Dreams of a Final Theory.* New York: Pantheon, 1992.

Whitehead, Alfred North. *Modes of Thought.* New York: Free Press, 1968.

Whitehead, Alfred North. *Religion in the Making.* 1926. Reprint, Cleveland: World, 1960.

Wilson, Edward O. *On Human Nature.* New York: Bantam, 1978.

Wright, Robert. *The Evolution of God.* New York: Little, Brown, and Company, 2009.

Wuthnow, Robert. *After Heaven: Spirituality in America Since the 1950s.* Berkeley: University of California Press, 1998.

Yancey, Philip, "Dark Nature: The Prophets of Evolutionary Biology Want to Reduce Us to Mere Survival Machines." *Books and Culture*, March 1, 1998.

Zacharias, Ravi. *The Real Face of Atheism.* Grand Rapids: Baker Books, 2004.

Zaehner, R. C. *Hindu and Muslim Mysticism.* Oxford: Oneworld, 1960.

CPSIA information can be obtained at www.ICGtesting.com
Printed in the USA
LVOW12s1827281213

367243LV00004B/6/P

9 780764 822827